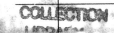

Wolfsbane

A Play

Georgina Reid

IF THIS PLAYSET IS RETURNED LATE –
BY EVEN ONE DAY –
A FULL REHIRE CHARGE IS PAYABLE

Samuel French – London
New York – Sydney – Toronto – Hollywood

© 1982 BY SAMUEL FRENCH LTD

ISBN 0 573 11503 6

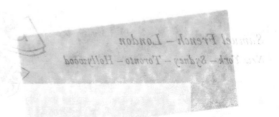

CHARACTERS

Joan Meredith
Luke Meredith
Howard Meredith
Gran (Mrs Blackwell)
Sarah Bond
Mrs Bond

The action takes place in the Merediths' kitchen

ACT I

ACT II

Time—the present

ACT I

SCENE 1

The Merediths' kitchen. A morning in September

It is a large, cheerful room which, in spite of its labour-saving equipment, does not lack character. There is a sink unit under a wide, cottage-type of window, with pot plants on the sill and a glimpse of the garden beyond. The furniture includes a Welsh dresser, an electric cooker, a refrigerator, a food cupboard and a kitchen unit with a toaster on it. There is a largish table C, flanked by three comfortable wooden chairs (one of these could be a rocking chair if there is room). There is a door to the garden up R and a door to the hall up L

When the CURTAIN *rises Joan Meredith, a good-looking, rather untidy woman of about forty-five, is leaning on the window sill sketching something outside. She is wearing a dressing-gown. The kettle is boiling and there is a great deal of smoke coming from the toaster*

After a moment Luke Meredith bursts in at the door L. *He is a pleasant youth of about twenty, wearing pyjamas with the top undone. He rushes across to the cooker, turns off the kettle and the toaster, dashes to the door* R *with the burnt toast and throws it out into the garden. He returns, fanning the air wildly with his arms, then stands grimly over his mother and addresses her loudly*

Luke Mother!
Joan (*still sketching*) Mm?
Luke (*grabbing her sketch book*) Mother!
Joan (*startled*) Oh! Wasn't that rather rude, dear?
Luke (*vehemently*) Yes.
Joan (*mildly*) Is something wrong?
Luke Well, I don't know if it's wrong but it's very irritating.
Joan What is?
Luke Seeing you standing there sketching while the kettle boils dry and the toast is burned to charcoal.
Joan Oh dear, is it? I'm so sorry, dear. I just happened to see this squirrel in the garden and I *had* to get it down on paper. Look, isn't it beautiful?
Luke (*with a brief glance*) Not half as beautiful as a plate of bacon and eggs.
Joan Oh, you poor thing, you're hungry. Look I must get on with this sketch; it's going to be part of that animal frieze I'm making for the children's chapel. (*She takes the sketch book back*) Why don't you fry yourself some bacon?
Luke Because the frying pan is full of blackened burnt onions—the

remains of Dad's attempt to cook his own supper last night. Look! (*He shows her the burnt frying pan*)

Joan Oh, I wondered what I could smell. If you can wait I'll clean it . . .

Luke Don't bother. The sight has taken away my appetite. I'll have some corn flakes. (*He gets the corn flakes from the cupboard, puts some into a bowl, sits at the table and adds milk, looks for the sugar, gets up again, gets the sugar from the dresser, sits, can't find a spoon, rises and fetches one from the dresser drawer*) I can't understand it. Do you know, there's a girl at college who regularly cooks a four-course dinner on a gas-ring in her bedroom. In this kitchen we have all the wonders of modern engineering, and you're never here long enough to boil an egg.

Joan Darling, I simply don't have time for cooking. I'm half-way through a really big commission and it's got to be finished by October. It's important.

Luke More important than feeding your family?

Joan Well, you're not starving, are you? There's always salads—and Gran is getting quite good at beans on toast.

Luke So she should be. She's done it every day for a fortnight.

Howard Meredith enters quietly from the door L. *He also is in a dressing-gown. He is about fifty, patient, sympathetic, with a touch of dryness in his humour*

Hello, Dad, guess what's for breakfast. Grey squirrel!

Howard (*looking over Joan's shoulder*) Splendid.

Joan He sat quite still for ages—posing for me—till Luke came in demanding food.

Luke Oh, I apologize for having a healthy appetite.

Joan (*going back to her sketching*) I bet your girl-friend with the gas-ring has never been commissioned to carve a portrait bust of the Prime Minister.

Luke All right, I grant you that. And don't think I'm not proud of you. I've dined out repeatedly on your fame as a sculptor. Only, right now, getting down to the basic urges, so to speak, I'd rather dine out on steak and kidney pudding. Do you know, I wake in the night, weeping and calling out for Mrs Larkins?

Howard Mrs Larkins? Was she the one who . . .?

Luke Yes, she was the one who made a gigantic steak and kidney pud every Saturday, and eventually went to Australia to help her daughter have a baby.

Howard Oh, that was Mrs Larkins, was it? Well, which was the one who plucked her eyebrows and wore her hair in a net?

Luke Golly, yes, that was Edie, wasn't it? Never knew her other name. Cooked everything in a frying pan and was heavy-handed with the pepper. What happened to her?

Howard begins to make a pot of tea

Howard Had a row with your grandmother, I expect. They mostly do, I notice.

Luke (*grinning*) Old battleaxe. I love watching her sail into battle, don't you? Were you there, that time she accused Mrs Pennycuik of pinching our groceries?

Howard Yes, confound it. Mrs Pennycuik was the best cook we ever had and I was proud to have her pinch our groceries. Your grandmother has lost us more cooks than I care to think of, and if she picks a quarrel with the next one . . .

Luke (*pleased*) Oh, have we engaged a new one?

Howard I imagine so. Your mother went up to London to the agency yesterday, didn't you dear?

Joan (*dragging her eyes away from her sketch book*) Mm? Didn't I what?

Howard Go up to the agency yesterday and engage a cook.

Joan looks aghast and claps a hand to her mouth

Joan Oh!

Luke Mother! You forgot!

Joan I went to an art exhibition and there was a terrible piece of sculpture called *Nemesis* and it drove everything else out of my head. I'm awfully sorry, darling. I'll go again next week.

Luke (*angrily*) Next week? You think I can live another week on baked beans and sardines? Have you no heart, woman?

Joan Perhaps Gran will make us a shepherd's pie.

Luke Gran makes a frightful shepherd's pie—it's like grey soup with a head on it. Your trouble is, you just don't notice what you're eating.

Howard Steady on, lad. Don't get excited.

Luke You'll drive us all from home. I mean it. I've written to Henry and begged him quite shamelessly to let me stay with them. Dad has to go down to the pub every time he wants a hot snack; Gran is driven to the O.P.D.C.—and you carry on hammering at a ton of granite and eating bread and cheese in blind oblivion! It's incredible!

He bangs out L

Howard (*peacefully pouring tea for two*) It puzzles me when people tell me that we suffer from the inability to communicate. It appears to me that our son communicates all too well. What is this O.P.D.C. that your mother is driven to? It sounds like the Russian secret police.

Joan It's the Old People's Day Centre. Pensioners can get a hot meal there very cheaply. Mother goes twice a week.

Howard Perhaps if I put on a false beard I could sneak in behind her.

Joan Howard, I'm sorry that I'm such a rotten housekeeper. It must be frightful being married to someone who turns out statues instead of tempting dishes. I should have warned you when you proposed to me that cooking comes way down on my list of priorities. And I forget all the important things and half the time I'm so absorbed in my work I don't even talk to you!

Howard That's not a vice, it's a virtue. A solicitor's life is beset with people who talk to him all day long. They queue up to pour out their eloquence into my long-suffering ears. It's sheer heaven to come home to my quiet wife.

Joan I was a very quiet child, I know. Probably because my mother was always arguing with my father.

Howard And the muscular strength that it gave to her jaw has lasted the rest of her life.

Joan (*smiling*) Yes, I'm afraid so.

Howard You never argue with her. Isn't that rather unkind when she so loves an argument?

Joan Maybe. But Luke's very good. He's always ready to take up the cudgels.

Howard Yes, they're two of a kind.

Gran (Mrs Blackwell), a brisk old lady of seventy, enters by the door R. *She is* not *in a dressing-gown. She is much smarter in her dress than Joan, her daughter*

Gran You're up at last then. Do you realize it's ten o'clock in the morning?

Howard I do. Can't a man have a lie-in on a Saturday?

Gran You miss the best of the morning. The garden is at its best while the dew is still on it.

Joan starts to pour her some tea

Is that tea or coffee?

Joan I don't know. (*She sniffs at it*) Tea, I think.

Gran Then don't bother. I can't stand that Indian stuff. Howard, you've got blackfly on the viburnum. Where's Luke? Still in bed?

Joan becomes immersed in her library book

Howard No. He's been in and had some corn flakes and gone again.

Gran Corn flakes? That's not enough for a growing boy.

Howard That's what he seemed to think too. He stamped out in a temper because Joan forgot to go and see about a cook yesterday.

Gran Really, Joan, I don't know what goes on in that head of yours. I suppose this means I shall have to make one of my shepherd's pies again.

Howard Is that the only recipe you know, Mother?

Gran It is. And I'm none too sure of that. One didn't learn these things when I was a girl. (*Brightening*) I shall have to ring the butcher. He'll be a bit cool with me, I expect, after the argument we had last week.

Howard You had an argument?

Gran Yes. I told him he'd given me short weight.

Howard And had he?

Gran Well, no. It turned out that Luke had given a large portion to Tiger Lily. However, I shan't admit it. One doesn't apologize to tradesmen.

Howard Minced beef is too good for a cat. You should get the butcher to send up some lights.

Gran I did, once. You should have seen the look on Tiger Lily's face! I never saw a cat look so insulted.

Luke enters L *with a letter and a newspaper*

Luke Morning, Gran. There's a letter for you, Mum. (*He puts the letter beside Joan's plate and opens the newspaper*)

Joan Thank you, dear.

Gran Luke, I don't consider you are properly dressed.

Luke I don't get a good example from my parents.

Gran They at least have on dressing gowns and are decently covered.

Luke So am I decently covered. My God, if you saw what some fellows wear at college . . .

Gran I don't care what you get up to at college. There, it's expected of you. Here, it is not, and if some gently-reared young virgin should come up the garden path and come face to face with you in your night attire . . .

Luke What gently-reared young virgins are you expecting?

Gran Well, the vicar keeps sending girls round to sit for your mother. They've none of them been very satisfactory but the vicar never gives up.

Joan (*staring at her letter*) I don't believe it!

Luke *What* don't you believe?

Joan I've engaged a cook!

Howard Well done! How did you find her?

Joan I've no idea.

Gran That's ridiculous.

Joan It seems that I wrote to her.

Gran And you don't remember?

Joan No.

Luke What's she called?

Joan (*consulting the letter*) Mrs Bond.

Luke That's perfect! (*Singing*)
"What shall we have for dinner, Mrs Bond?
There's beef in the larder and ducks on the pond."

Gran joins in and they dance together singing the chorus

Luke ⎱ (*together*) "Dilly-dilly, dilly-dilly, come and be killed!
Gran ⎰ Dilly-dilly, dilly-dilly, come and be killed!"

Howard Let's see. (*He takes the letter and reads aloud*) "Dear Mrs Meredith, Thank you for your letter of the tenth instant. I shall be pleased to cook for you and your family and shall endeavour to give every satisfaction. I shall arrive by the morning train on September fourteenth. Yours faithfully, Theresa Bond. P.S. Sarah can share my bed if necessary."

Gran Who on earth is Sarah? A cat?

Luke It sounds more like a kid, to me. A grubby little darling with tousled locks and a running nose.

Howard I think so too. Joan, how did you hear of this person?

Joan (*anxiously twisting her hands*) Let me think, let me think!

Howard "Your letter of the tenth instant." Where were you on the tenth? It was last Tuesday. Luke, look at the engagement calendar. Where was your mother on Tuesday?

Luke (*consulting the calendar on the wall* R) At the dentist.

Joan At the dentist? Oh—yes, the dentist, of course. You know how they have lots of magazines to keep you from going crazy while you wait? It was in one of those that I saw this advertisement and to while away the time I scribbled a letter. I suppose I must have posted it later on, though I don't remember putting a stamp on it.

Howard But what did the advertisement say?

Joan I don't remember. Just that she wanted a residential post. "Good, experienced, family cook" I think it said.

Gran But this Sarah; did the advertisement mention a child?

Joan I don't think so. I'm not really sure.

Howard Look, Joan, I'm reasonably fond of children but I don't want to be saddled with a toddler. It would roam all over the house and get its sticky fingers into everything.

Joan She might get into my studio. There are dangerous tools in there—or something might fall on her.

Luke My God, how can I be expected to study with a toddler clinging round my knees?

Gran Yes, very tiresome. And small children are always catching measles or chicken-pox and break out into a rash for no reason at all. I think you had better write straight away and tell her you've changed your mind and don't want her.

Joan Yes, I suppose so.

Howard I don't think there's time for you to write a letter.

Gran Why? What's today?

Luke (*consulting the calendar*) The fourteenth.

Howard (*reading the letter*) "I shall arrive by the morning train on September fourteenth."

Luke Cripes! She's coming today!

Howard On the morning train!

Joan But she can't!

Luke I bet that even now she's trudging up the road with your letter in one hand and little Sarah's sticky paw in the other.

Joan Whatever shall I tell her?

Gran Say you've changed your mind.

Joan She'll think me a fool.

Howard Say the post has been filled already.

Joan How can I say that? I offered her the job—I think.

Luke Dear God, don't you *know*?

Joan Oh Luke, don't be so hard. I was thinking mostly about the dentist and quaking with fear at the prospect. All I can tell you is that I *think* I offered her the job, and her letter bears it out.

Luke Well, say that Dad's been offered a post in America and we're all moving abroad in ten days' time.

Joan I shall blush and stammer. I'm no good at telling lies.

There is a loud peal at the door bell, off L

(*With a loud gasp*) She's come!

Howard Don't look so terrified. It may not be Mrs Bond. It may be one of the vicar's virgins.

Luke I'll have a peep. (*He opens the door* L *a crack and shuts it again*) It's
her all right, staring in through the stained-glass door with sad, accusing
eyes.

Joan Howard, we're both in our dressing gowns. We can't go to the door
like this at ten o'clock in the morning.

Luke Don't look at *me*. I'm barely decent.

Gran (*taking a deep determined breath*) It looks as though *I* shall have to
deal with her.

Joan Oh, Mother, will you really? You're wonderful.

Luke What will you tell her?

Gran What you suggested. That we're all going to America in ten days'
time. And don't you three show yourselves or she'll think this is a home
for convalescent half-wits.

Gran exits L

Luke God bless the old battleaxe.

Howard Luke, will you please show more respect for your grandmother.

Luke I have every respect for my grandmother. Next to Mrs Larkins she's
my favourite person. I wish I could hear what she says. (*He opens the
door a crack again*)

Joan What are they doing?

Luke They're standing in the middle of the hall, confronting each other.
She's rather a formidable looking woman, all dressed in black.

Joan Oh dear, I'm glad I don't have to face her.

Howard Where's the child?

Luke Not in sight. Probably outside, sitting on a cabin trunk and sucking
a lollipop.

Howard I just hope the little perisher isn't picking my dahlias.

Joan Oh dear, I feel badly about this. It's all my fault.

Howard I blame the dentist. He has no right to put out magazines that are
less than three months old.

Luke Mrs Bond is flourishing a letter—Mum's letter, no doubt. She's gone
rather red in face. Grandmother is gravely composed. I fancy she's
saying "my good woman". I'd never have the nerve to say "my good
woman" to a total stranger.

Howard Hush. Don't talk so much. I want to hear what they're saying.

Joan (*crossing to the window and looking out*) Oh don't, I can't bear it. I'd
like to bury my head in the sand until she's gone away.

Luke (*closing the door*) Do you realize we may be turning away the world's
best cook?

Howard That's a risk I am prepared to take.

Luke Maybe we could persuade her to send Sarah to a boarding school.

Howard They don't have boarding schools for toddlers. It's no good,
Luke, we must face another week of shepherd's pie.

Luke Like hell! I'm going to stay with Henry.

Joan There's someone in the garden.

Howard The man with the peat?

Joan No, a young woman.

They all look out

Howard Perhaps she's coming to model for you, Joan. You asked the vicar to find someone, didn't you?

Joan I hope she is. She looks quite promising. I've been itching to start work on a new head.

Howard She looks a bit lost. Hadn't you better ask her in?

Joan (*indicating her dressing gown*) Like this?

Luke Oh, good Lord, Mother, *she's* coming to pose for *you*, not vice versa. I'll keep in the background, or drape a towel across my torso.

Joan opens the door R

Joan (*calling*) Good-morning. Won't you come in?

Sarah Bond enters. She is sixteen years old, rather thin and pale but with fine features. Her clothes are plain and her hair is rather severe in style, but she has a delightful smile. Her manner is a mixture of shyness and frankness which is very appealing

Sarah Good-morning. I hope you didn't mind me walking round the garden. It's a beautiful garden. I never saw such dahlias.

Joan Yes, my husband is very proud of them. I'm Joan Meredith—(*she shakes hands*)—and this is my husband and my son, Luke.

Sarah (*shyly*) How do you do. I'm Sarah Bond.

There is a stunned silence as they take this in

Howard Sarah Bond? You're the daughter of—of Mrs Bond? (*He gestures vaguely towards the hall*)

Sarah Yes. I was supposed to wait outside. That's what I always do.

Luke Why?

Sarah They always want to tell my mother about the things I mustn't do, like banging doors and leaving a tide mark in the bath and playing the wireless too loud. I find it less embarrassing to wait outside until that's over.

There is a pause

Howard Won't you sit down?

Sarah (*sitting on the edge of the chair*) Thank you. What a lovely big kitchen. Mother will enjoy working here, and I'll be able to do my homework here without getting in anyone's way.

Joan Homework? Where do you go to school?

Sarah I suppose I shall go to the local one. I usually do. I've been to five different schools since I was thirteen.

Howard How old are you now?

Sarah Sixteen and a bit.

Luke We thought you'd be younger.

Sarah smiles and looks about her

We thought you'd be a *lot* younger.

Sarah (*looking worried*) I hope you're not thinking that I'll eat a lot. I've really got a very small appetite, and Mother always accepts lower wages so as to pay for my board and lodging. (*Their silence worries her*) At the week-ends I'd do housework for you, and run errands. I could weed the garden too. I'm very fond of gardening. (*After a pause*) I'm sorry you thought I was so much younger.

Howard No, no, it's just a misunderstanding. Your mother said in her letter that you could share her bed, so we thought that . . .

Sarah Oh yes, I don't mind a bit. I've often had to sleep in Mother's bed. Honestly, it doesn't worry us at all. I'm rather thin, you see, so I don't take up a lot of room. (*After an uncomfortable pause*) Where's Mother? Is the mistress showing her the house?

Joan Er—no. My mother is talking to her in the hall.

Sarah You wait till she sees this super kitchen. She won't show that she's pleased but I shall know. I can always tell when Mother's pleased. She's been so much happier since she had your letter. Things had been bad for her up till then. She hadn't been sleeping much at night, worrying, you know. But she prayed a lot, and when your letter came she said it was like the answer to a prayer.

Luke Miss Bond, can your mother make a good steak and kidney pudding?

Sarah Of course she can. My mother makes superb steak and kidney puddings. Everything she cooks is wonderful. You'll grow fat on her cooking.

Howard (*smiling*) *You* haven't grown fat on it.

Sarah No, I don't seem to repay good feeding. I think I take after my father. He was very thin, as far as I can remember.

Joan (*diffidently*) When I saw you, I thought you were coming to model for me.

Sarah To model?

Joan To sit for me. I'm a sculptor. Have you ever been a model?

Sarah Oh no. I'm too plain.

Joan No, you have a good head. An excellent head. Howard, this child's head is what I've always wanted—for my *Aphrodite*. The vicar keeps sending me girls that are too thickset and earthy, when what I want is something more—spiritual. I've been looking for a model like this for ages and ages and I'd nearly given up hope.

Sarah I'd be delighted to sit for you, Mrs Meredith, as often as you like.

Joan (*pleadingly*) Howard, couldn't we . . .?

Howard (*patting her arm*) Perhaps we could if it's not too late.

A door is closed firmly, off L

Luke That's the door. You *are* too late.

Joan You mean . . .?

Luke I mean that Gran has done what you asked her to do.

Joan Oh no!

Gran enters L, *grimly triumphant*

Gran Hah! That's that.

Joan You mean, she's gone?

Gran At last. It took a long time to convince her, and when I said you were
going to America she looked positively sceptical.

Sarah Going to America?

Gran Who's this?

Luke Grandmother, this is Sarah. Sarah Bond.

Sarah How do you do.

Gran But—but she's not a toddler!

Sarah No, I'm not. Does it matter?

Gran It ... No, it doesn't make the slightest difference. Mr and Mrs
Meredith are off to America in a fortnight. I'm sorry, child, but you've
come all this way for nothing. It's most unfortunate. Your mother is
waiting for you outside, so perhaps you'd better go. (*She goes to the door*
R *and opens it*)

Sarah (*in anguish*) Mrs Meredith!

Joan (*in desperation*) Howard!

Howard (*crossing and shutting the door*) Mother, we've changed our
minds. We don't want Sarah to go. We don't want her mother to go.

Gran (*indignantly*) What! Why, you—you crew of back-sliding hypocrites!
You let me go out there and turn that woman away; you let me expose
myself to recriminations, reproaches, entreaties—a more unpleasant
experience I have never encountered——

Joan I'm sorry, Mother.

Gran —and now you stand there and say you've revoked!

Joan Mother, I *must* have Sarah, to sit for me. She's exactly what I've been
looking for. She's the perfect Aphrodite.

Gran (*looking at Sarah more closely*) Aphrodite! She looks nothing but a
schoolgirl to me.

Joan She's so much more than that. I'll never find such a head again.

Howard (*decisively*) Sarah, please go and ask your mother to come back
and see me. Tell her there's been a mistake.

Sarah hurries to obey

And Sarah, don't mention this modelling business for the time being, eh?

Sarah No, sir.

Sarah exits R

Gran (*very angry*) Now look here, Howard, I resent being made to look a
fool in this way.

Joan Oh Mother, I'm terribly sorry.

Gran Being sorry doesn't help at all. I'm furious with you both, getting me
to do your dirty work, and all for nothing. How do you explain this—
this change of heart?

Howard I shall endeavour to put all the blame on myself. Your integrity
shall be upheld, come what may.

Gran You'll need all your eloquence to convince this one. She's got a very
suspicious look in her eye. And she speaks her mind too. Quite honestly,
Joan, I found her rather intimidating.

Joan Intimidating? How do you mean?

Gran You'll find out. It's too late now, of course—you've set your heart on Sarah I can see—but I hope you realize you're taking on this woman without any references?
Howard No references?
Gran None. She says they were destroyed in a fire.
Joan Well, if that's so she can't be expected to have references.
Gran Huh, *if* it's true.
Luke Didn't you *like* Mrs Bond, Grandmother?
Gran No, Luke, and I'm quite certain she didn't like me. If looks could kill, I wouldn't have come out of that encounter alive. By the way, Howard, make sure she gives you back the five pounds I paid her for her travelling expenses. And where is that girl going to sleep?
Joan We could put the small divan in her mother's room.
Luke Why can't she have my study? There's a bed in there. I can do my work downstairs.
Joan That's very kind of you dear, but not really necessary.
Luke (*determinedly*) I *want* her to have my study.

They stare at him and he looks sheepish

Well, you heard what she said: always having to share her mother's room, sometimes even the same bed. When a girl gets to that age she ought to have a place of her own. I bet she's never had her own bedroom.
Joan Well, perhaps you're right. It'll be next door to her mother's room, and it has a nice view of the church.
Gran Oh, that's another thing. She's religious. She says things like "God has seen fit to humble me".
Luke Christ! I shall have to stop swearing. What a price to pay!
Gran It's too late to think of that. Well, I'll go up and sort out some clean sheets.
Howard Won't you stay and give me moral support?
Gran What? Sit meekly by while you explain that your mother-in-law is a senile old fool with delusions about trips to America? Not likely. I'm afraid you have permanently soured my relationship with Mrs Bond.

Gran exits L

Howard Oh dear, that's a bad beginning.
Luke I don't know. It might be the best thing.
Howard What might?
Luke If Gran and Mrs Bond aren't on speaking terms. Less chance of argument. More peace and joy and lovely food.
Howard I thought you were going to stay with Henry.
Luke Not likely. I hate staying with Henry. The food is good but his father is a political bore. I tell you what, I'll go and start clearing out my study.
Joan Yes, do, dear.

Luke exits L

(*Making useless dabs at her hair*) Goodness, I don't think I've combed my hair this morning. Whatever will the woman think?

Howard Who cares what the woman thinks? A famous sculptress like you is expected to be somewhat eccentric. And anyway, you look perfectly beautiful.

Joan Here they come.

Sarah enters R, *followed by her mother. Mrs Bond is about fifty years old, sad-eyed, cold and formal in her manner, and has a way of setting her mouth which suggests a strong will. She is dressed in black clothes and wears an uncompromising hat*

Howard (*going forward to shake hands, full of warmth and charm*) Do come in, Mrs Bond. I'm Howard Meredith and this is my wife.

Mrs Bond touches his hand briefly

Now, it looks as though there has been an unfortunate mistake.

Mrs Bond Indeed, sir?

Howard I believe my wife wrote and offered you a job here as our cook, am I right?

Mrs Bond So I understood. But another lady has just informed me that I am not wanted and that you are all going to America.

Howard All a misunderstanding, I'm afraid. I was *offered* a job in America, but I turned it down. Unfortunately I forgot to tell my mother-in-law.

Sarah And you're not going to America?

Howard Definitely not.

Sarah There you are, Mother. What did I tell you?

Mrs Bond Does this mean you wish me to remain as your cook?

Howard Most certainly.

Mrs Bond And the lady who wrote me the letter?

Joan I wrote the letter, Mrs Bond.

Mrs Bond You wish me to remain?

Joan Oh yes, *please*, if you will.

Mrs Bond I have no references. There was a fire at my last place of residence.

Howard Then we shall have to take your cooking on trust.

Mrs Bond I am a very good cook. I have worked for ambassadors and dignitaries of the church. However, I normally accept a lower wage than is normal for someone of my experience. This is because of my daughter, Sarah.

Howard I'm sure we shall be able to agree on a suitable salary.

Mrs Bond Sarah is a quiet child and has learned the need to be self-effacing in other people's homes.

Howard She sounds an admirable young person. Luckily we have a spare bedroom for her, next door to yours.

Mrs Bond There is no need. She has always shared my room.

Sarah Oh Mother, a room of my own! Please, please let me! Or will it be an extra expense?

Howard By no means. Expense doesn't enter into it. The room is there so why not use it?

Sarah Oh, thank you, Mr Meredith. Thank you, Mrs Meredith. It'll be wonderful.

Joan It's quite small, I'm afraid.

Sarah That doesn't matter. I shall love it. Shall I take my case up, Mother?

Mrs Bond (*sharply*) No. I have not yet decided whether to take the post.

Sarah (*taken aback*) Not yet . . . but Mother, you must. It's lovely here. Look at this marvellous big kitchen. And besides, we've nowhere else to go.

Mrs Bond Be silent, child. I must know in my heart that the Lord has guided me here. The strange reception that greeted us has filled me with doubts.

Howard But that was just a misunderstanding. My mother-in-law is very embarrassed about it and hopes you won't think she has a personal grudge against you.

Mrs Bond Personal grudge? Is there any reason why she should?

Howard Of course not. How could she?

Mrs Bond There was a feeling passed between us, as though she did not trust me.

Howard Oh, take no notice of that, Mrs Bond. My mother-in-law doesn't trust anyone, not even me. Feelings are always passing between us. I no longer worry about it.

Mrs Bond Are there no other members of the family?

Howard Only my son, Luke. He's up at Cambridge most of the time, but home now for the long vacation, and simply yearning to sample your cooking.

Mrs Bond Young men of that age make me nervous. They are often loud and violent.

Howard Oh, Luke's not loud and violent. He's not really a typical student type. He's more . . .

Luke enters L *rather precipitately, with an armful of books. He trips over and falls to his knees scattering books on the floor*

Luke (*loudly*) Bloody hell!

Howard (*sternly*) Luke! Kindly do not use that language in front of ladies!

Luke (*on his knees, gathering up books*) Oh, sorry. I was turning out some of my old school books and I thought they might be useful to Sarah.

Howard For heaven's sake, leave the books and go and put some clothes on.

Luke Just a minute, Dad. Look, Sarah, there's a complete Shakespeare and a couple of poetry books and an atlas and . . .

Howard Luke! Go and put some clothes on!

Luke I've got some clothes on. You talk as if I were going round starkers.

Howard Just for once in your life, don't argue.

Howard takes the books from Luke and pushes him out of the door L

Luke exits L

Sorry about that, Mrs Bond. From now on I'll see that young Luke observes the proprieties.

Mrs Bond While the young man is at home, Sarah will share my bedroom.

Sarah But Mother . . .

Mrs Bond Don't argue, Sarah. You may use the other room while he is away at college.

Howard Hang it all, Mrs Bond, my son is quite trustworthy with young women.

Mrs Bond I hope so, sir. I have no wish to offend you, but my daughter's good name is invaluable.

Joan You're quite right, Mrs Bond. If Howard had a daughter of his own, he'd be every bit as careful of her. Does this mean that you are going to stay?

Mrs Bond I must have time off every Sunday to go to Divine Service.

Joan Of course.

Mrs Bond (*taking a deep breath*) In that case, I will see the room that you have allotted to us. Sarah, you will remain here while money matters are discussed.

Sarah Yes, Mother.

Joan I'll show you the way.

Joan goes out L, followed by Mrs Bond

Howard D'you think she'll decide in our favour?

Sarah (*seriously*) I expect so. As long as she can see the hand of God in it.

Howard Oh. Do you suppose she will? I felt that when Luke made his entrance, the hand of God had put its foot in it.

Sarah (*giggling*) That's a mixed metaphor, isn't it? We did them at my last school. (*More seriously*) I hope you won't make fun of religion when Mother's here. It upsets her. She feels rather strongly about it.

Howard Your mother seems a very strong-minded woman.

Sarah Yes, she's had to be. My father deserted her when I was quite a baby and she's had a hard time. Sometimes she sounds a bit severe but in fact she's terribly good to me. I can't bear it when people upset her.

Howard Now, don't worry, child. Nobody's going to upset your mother. Where shall we put these books? How about the bottom shelf of the dresser?

Sarah Yes, that'll be handy when I do my homework. The Shakespeare is bound to be useful. What are the poets?

Howard This is my favourite, Keats. Like his stuff?

Sarah I think so. He wrote a lot about Nature, didn't he?

Howard Yes, but it wasn't wishy-washy stuff. It was intense and dramatic.

Sarah opens the book and reads at random

Sarah "No, no, go not to Lethe, neither twist
　　　Wolf's-bane, tight-rooted, for its poisonous wine ..."

Howard That's his *Ode On Melancholy*.

Sarah I don't really understand it. Who was Lethe?

Howard You mean, *what* was Lethe? Lethe was the river of forgetfulness.

Sarah Keats was a chemist's assistant, wasn't he? That's what my mother used to be. When she was a girl, I mean. Her father was a chemist and she used to help in the shop. He taught her a lot about medicines and pills and poisons, but in the end she decided she'd rather be a cook.

Howard And what would *you* like to be?

Sarah An actress. I love acting and reading plays and poetry. I shall learn some of Keats and mutter it to myself when I'm feeling melancholy.

Howard I mutter poetry too. I'm too conventional to say it out loud. It's not the sort of thing a discreet solicitor should do.

Gran enters from the garden holding a parcel of fish

Gran I met the fishmonger bringing Tiger Lily's weekly rations.

Sarah Tiger Lily? That's a character in *Peter Pan*, isn't it?

Gran Yes, child. And it's also a big, fat, ginger cat with fixed ideas about diet. (*She puts the fish on a plate and places it in the refrigerator*)

Sarah How splendid. Where is she?

Howard Her favourite place is the dining-room table.

Sarah May I go and look at her? I love cats. Mother hates them, I'm afraid. I hope Tiger Lily won't upset her.

Sarah exits L

Gran and Howard begin to clear the table, leaving the milk jug and sugar bowl

Howard That poor child seems to live in constant dread that something might upset her mother.

Gran Having met the mother, that doesn't surprise me. She'd put arsenic in your soup without turning a hair.

Howard I think we ought to tread warily. We don't want her to walk out in a huff, do we?

Gran Don't we? I wouldn't mind.

Howard Mother, I know that you and Mrs Bond had an unfortunate introduction, but I do want you to be careful not to—well—rub her up the wrong way.

Gran Howard, I have yet to see the day when I will kotow to a cook. I'm surprised to learn that your gluttonous appetites have overcome your pride and self-respect.

Howard Neither my pride nor my gluttony have anything to do with it. I want that woman to remain here under this roof for as long as Joan has need of her daughter.

Gran Oh, that statue.

Howard Yes, that statue. Joan is your daughter; you must know how she feels about her work.

Gran It's the only thing she lives for.

Howard Precisely. Do you know, Mother, that in all our married life, Joan has never asked me a favour?

Gran I can quite believe it. Joan doesn't ask for favours.

Howard Not until this morning. But she saw in Sarah Bond the model she has been searching for, and she feared she was going to lose her. So she turned to me and begged for help, for the first time in her life. Naturally I am not going to let her down—and neither are you.

Gran (*rather hurt*) As if I would. To hear you talk, one would think I was a quarrelsome old hag.

Howard (*smiling*) Of course you're not, Mother.

Gran I shall praise Mrs Bond's cooking even if it kills me.

Howard That's the spirit.

Gran And between meals I shall give her a wide berth. It's a pity one has to pass through the kitchen in order to reach the back garden.

Howard You could go round the front.

Mrs Bond enters L, *without her hat and coat and carrying her apron. She closes the door and stands looking at them expressionlessly*

Ah, Mrs Bond. Everything settled? Bedroom satisfactory? Wages sufficient?

Mrs Bond Yes thank you, sir. (*She turns to Gran*) And here is the money you gave me for my return journey. (*She offers the five-pound note*)

Gran (*taking it*) Oh. Thank you.

Howard Then I take it you are staying?

Mrs Bond (*nodding*) God willing.

Howard Good. I expect you will want to have time to unpack.

Mrs Bond I have unpacked my apron, sir. (*She ties it on*) That's all that is necessary. Lunch will be at one o'clock, if that suits you.

Howard Good heavens, are you going to conjure up a meal out of thin air?

Mrs Bond I had assumed there would be food in the house.

Gran (*flatly*) There's some fresh cod fillet in the refrigerator, but that's for the cat. There's nothing else.

Mrs Bond (*turning and looking at her*) You buy fresh cod fillet for the cat and nothing for yourselves?

Gran It's a standing order. The fishmonger brings it every Saturday.

Mrs Bond Have you potatoes?

Gran Yes.

Mrs Bond Then I shall cook fish and chips for your lunch.

Howard Oh splendid, my favourite dish.

Gran But what about Tiger Lily?

Mrs Bond (*coldly*) Tiger Lily?

Gran The cat. What will she have if we eat her fish?

Mrs Bond This afternoon I shall go shopping and while I am at the butcher's I will purchase some lights or similar offal for the cat. Surely that is better than wasting good food on animals that do nothing to earn it?

Howard I quite agree.

Gran If it comes to that, *I* do nothing to earn *my* food. Am I to be given lights or similar offal?

Howard Nonsense, Mother, you're a most useful member of the household. Now, come along. Mrs Bond will want to have the kitchen to herself.

Howard and Gran move to leave

Mrs Bond With regard to Tiger Lily—I presume you are referring to the large ginger cat at present asleep on the dining-room table?

Howard Yes.

Mrs Bond I really think it would be better if the animal were not allowed on a table where food is served. Cats are often verminous—especially the long-haired variety.

Gran (*indignantly*) Tiger Lily is not verminous! I've had that cat for twelve years and she's never had a flea!

Howard Mother, suppose you come and show me that blackfly on the viburnum.

Gran Tiger Lily is not verminous.

Howard Of course not. Mrs Bond hasn't yet had a chance to find out what a remarkably clean and healthy cat she is.

Gran She certainly is.

Mrs Bond I am pleased to hear it. Nevertheless, I'd rather she didn't set foot in the kitchen.

Howard (*hastily*) Very wise. Very wise. I'm glad to know that you are so keen on hygiene. Come along, Mother, we shall have to act fast if we're to stop the blackfly spreading to the nasturtiums.

Howard and Gran exit into the garden

Mrs Bond looks grimly satisfied. She stands by the window and turns up her sleeves as—

the CURTAIN *falls*

SCENE 2

The same. A fortnight later

Luke, fully dressed, is at the cooker making a pot of coffee. After a moment Howard peers round the door L

Howard Do I smell coffee?

Luke Only this instant stuff. I can't make the real thing like Mrs Bond does.

Howard (*coming in*) Never mind. It makes a nice change to have the kitchen to ourselves and muck around without her disapproving glare. (*He puts four cups and saucers on a tray and takes it to the table*) What time does she get back from church?

Luke Depends on who's preaching. If it's the vicar we should be safe for another half-hour.

Howard Safe? To drink instant coffee in one's own kitchen? Surely we don't have to feel guilty about that?

Luke Don't we? I've felt guilty ever since that woman arrived. (*He pours coffee for two*)

Howard Guilty of what?

Luke God knows.

They sit down

That, for instance. Taking the name of the Lord thy God in vain. I'm always doing it. She looks at me as if she's counting the number of times I've broken the commandments and reporting back to Head Office.

Howard But, surely she must approve of the way you enjoy your meals?

Luke You'd think so, wouldn't you? It's all so bloody marvellous, I can't help asking for more, and finishing every scrap on the plate, and instead of a look of approval I can see contempt in her eye. She thinks I'm a gluttonous pig. And do you know that while we are feeding like fighting cocks, she and Sarah are out here in the kitchen having a poached egg on toast!

Howard It's incredible. I spoke to her about that and she quoted something from the Bible about "a dinner of herbs where love is"—you know the bit.

Luke Love? I don't see much love between those two.

Howard Don't be misled by appearances, Luke. I know Mrs Bond seems hard on Sarah sometimes, but have you seen the way she looks at the girl when no-one is watching?

Luke She won't let anyone else look at her, though. As soon as I come into the room she finds some excuse to send Sarah away. It's ridiculous, as if I'm going to make obscene gestures or something. She'll end up with a thoroughly neurotic daughter.

Howard I shouldn't worry. Sarah seems a nice, normal child to me.

Joan enters L, *wearing a smudged smock*

Hello darling, come and have some coffee. How's the statue?

Joan Taking shape splendidly. Sarah's a very good model; she has a wonderful talent for repose.

Howard That probably comes of living all her life in other people's houses. She's had to sit still and keep quiet all the time.

Joan I came down to see if she's back from church. I thought we might have a session before lunch.

Luke (*pouring coffee*) Here, try this, Mother. I made it myself.

Joan Has anyone seen my library book? I've been looking for it for days. I forget the title—something about a body, I believe. (*She drinks her coffee*)

Luke They usually are.

Howard I can tell you where your library books are. Mrs Bond has locked them all in the sideboard and given me the key.

Luke Well! How's that for a high-handed old cow?

Joan But, good heavens, why?

Howard She considers them improper reading matter and doesn't wish her daughter to be contaminated by them.

Joan Contaminated? They couldn't contaminate a child of three!

Howard Blood and violence and sudden death?

Joan There's worse in *Grimm's Fairy Tales*—or the Bible for that matter. Oh really, it's too bad. If she weren't such a marvellous cook, I'd—I'd . . .

Luke Oh no, you wouldn't, you know. Even if her pastry was like lead, you'd still keep her, and you know it.

Joan Yes, I suppose so. For Sarah's sake.

Howard How a woman like that produced such a delightful child, I don't know. She must take after her father. (*He drinks*) She likes it here, you know, Sarah does. She's looking rosier—healthier. I met her yesterday, down by the river, with her arms full of blue flowers, and she looked a picture.

Luke I can see *you* don't regret the day they came.

Howard Do *you*?

Luke My inner man rejoices, every time I contemplate the next meal, but I can't help feeling I've sold my birthright for a mess of potage.

Joan Darling, do try and stand it for a few weeks. This head of Aphrodite is going to be the best thing I've ever done.

Luke Oh, I can stand it, but I have my doubts about Gran. It's only a matter of time before we have a battle of wills between her and Mrs Bond. I can see it brewing up.

Joan Oh, why are people so difficult? *I* don't mind Mrs Bond's eccentricities.

Luke (*smiling*) Mother, *you* wouldn't mind if you had to live with Frankenstein's Monster, so long as you could get on with your sculpture.

Sarah enters from the garden, wearing her school hat and blazer which she rapidly sheds

Sarah (*pleased*) Oh, you're all here in the kitchen. Were you having a solemn conclave?

Howard By no means. We're having elevenses. Won't you come and join us?

Sarah How lovely! Mother never has elevenses. But after singing five hymns and a psalm, I feel as dry as a desert.

Luke (*pouring coffee for her*) It'll be half cold, I expect.

Sarah (*taking a sip*) Oh no, it's just right. Do you know, that last hymn had ten verses and each one had a chorus. And half way through it, the organ gave out and we had to carry on without it, getting flatter and flatter. It was ghastly.

Howard Is your mother with you?

Sarah No, she stayed behind for communion. I'm supposed to be seeing to the dinner. (*She rises and goes to the cooker*) It's all ready. I've only got to turn things on and put the pie in the oven and then I'll be free to come and sit for you, Mrs Meredith. (*She adjusts the saucepans*) Mother doesn't actually know I sit for you. She thinks I just come over to watch you.

Joan Would she mind if she knew?

Sarah (*getting a pie from the refrigerator*) She might. It's hard to tell. It might come under the heading of Graven Images and then she'd put a stop to it and I'd be awfully disappointed. I love having my head modelled. Nobody has ever admired my head before. (*She puts the pie in the oven*) Sometimes I think my mother is over-protective towards me, but she can't help it. All mothers are the same.

Luke Oh no they aren't. My mother never felt a protective instinct in her life.

Sarah (*shocked*) Luke!

Luke It's perfectly true, isn't it, Mother? Did you ever feel protective towards me, even when I was little?

Joan (*vaguely*) I don't really remember, dear.

Sarah Oh, of course she did. It's a natural instinct. Why, a mother would even sacrifice her life to save her child.

Luke gives a rude laugh

It's true I tell you. Look at the animal kingdom: a tigress will defend her young to the death.

Luke Any likeness between my mother and a tigress is purely imaginary.

Sarah But she needn't *look* like a tigress, you silly. It's one of the facts of life. A mother will do anything to defend her child. Look, suppose you'd been bitten by a snake, your mother would suck out the poison, wouldn't she?

Luke No. She'd say, "Oh, what a beautiful snake. I must draw it."

Sarah Now you're being silly. Look, if you did something awful, like selling military secrets to a foreign power, your mother would suffer terribly but she wouldn't give you away.

Luke Wouldn't you, Mother?

Joan Wouldn't I what, dear?

Luke Tell the police that I was a Russian spy.

Joan But you're not, are you? I think I'll go and get on with some work. Come if you can, Sarah, but not if your mother needs you.

Joan exits L

Sarah She isn't offended, is she?

Luke Good heavens, no. She probably didn't even take in what we were talking about. Too busy thinking about her sculpture.

Sarah She loves her work, doesn't she?

Howard It's better than food and drink to her.

Sarah Not like Luke then. Food and drink are all he cares about. Oh Luke, you should have been in church this morning. The sermon was just meant for you. (*She looks at them over imaginary spectacles and imitates the vicar's sanctimonious manner*) "Ah, my friends, although you are here to listen to the word of the Lord, how many of you are already letting your thoughts dwell on the succulent roast beef awaiting you for Sunday lunch?"

Mrs Bond enters R unseen by the others. She pauses with her hand on the door knob

"How many of you have given up sober meditation of things spiritual, in order to anticipate the gluttonous delights of the flesh . . ."

Mrs Bond closes the door sharply and they all start. Their smiles fade and Sarah loses her look of vivacity

(*Guiltily*) Oh, Mother, we were just having a cup of coffee.

Mrs Bond (*without expression*) So I see.

Sarah Mrs Meredith was here, too, until a moment ago. Luke made the coffee and Mr Meredith asked me to join them.

Mrs Bond My kitchen is hardly the best place for family gatherings. In future I will serve coffee in the lounge as soon as I return from church. Now, Sarah, get these cups washed up and put away.

Sarah gathers up the cups, saucers and coffee pot and takes them to the sink. She gets the kettle from the cooker and pours water into the basin

And Mr Luke, if you don't mind, I'm going to need this table.
Luke (*rising*) Oh, all right, I'm going.

Luke bangs out angrily R

Howard I'll help dry the cups, Sarah. (*He takes the tea towel off the hook near the sink*)
Mrs Bond (*obviously displeased but trying not to show it*) Now, Mr Meredith, I really cannot allow that.
Howard (*starting to dry the cups*) But I helped to make them dirty.
Mrs Bond Nevertheless, the master of the house is not expected to do menial tasks. Please allow Sarah to do it for herself.
Howard (*blandly*) I'm sure you must want to go and take off your hat and coat, Mrs Bond. Sarah and I will be quite happy in our menial task.

Mrs Bond appears to swell with anger. She hesitates

Gran enters L, *looking worried*

Gran I'm sorry to intrude but has anyone seen my cat?
Mrs Bond No, I have not.
Howard Didn't she sleep in last night?
Gran No, she rarely does in warm weather.
Howard But, didn't she turn up for breakfast?
Gran No, and that's what worries me. She never fails to come for her breakfast. You don't think she's fallen in the river, do you?
Howard Of course not, Mother. More likely she's got shut in the airing cupboard.
Mrs Bond *That* she isn't. I found her there once but I made sure she'd never go there again.
Sarah Don't worry, Mrs Blackwell. I'll go and search for her in a few minutes.
Gran Thank you dear, but I rather think that Joan is waiting for you. You'd better not put that off.
Mrs Bond Put what off, Mrs Blackwell?
Gran Sitting for Joan.
Mrs Bond I don't understand. Why should Mrs Meredith require my daughter to sit?

Sarah and Howard look at each other apprehensively

Howard My wife is making a model of Sarah's head, Mrs Bond. It's a charming little thing. I think you'll like it.
Mrs Bond Sarah, how long has this been going on?
Sarah Only about a week, Mother.
Mrs Bond And did nobody think to ask my permission?
Sarah We didn't think you'd mind.

Howard My wife is a very gifted and notable sculptor, Mrs Bond. It's quite an honour to sit for her.

Mrs Bond An honour? Filling the child with conceit and vanity? Encouraging her to think herself something special?

Sarah (*anxiously*) I don't, Mother. I know I'm plain and ordinary. It hasn't made me vain, I promise.

Mrs Bond Hm. Didn't I see you looking at yourself in the glass this morning, and smiling as vain as any peacock?

Gran Surely a pretty girl can look at her reflection without committing a sin?

Mrs Bond "Everyone that is proud in heart is an abomination unto the Lord."

Gran Fiddlesticks.

Howard Mother, please.

Mrs Bond Whether it is vain or not, it is certainly immodest.

Sarah It's only a head and shoulders, Mother.

Mrs Bond And are the shoulders clothed?

Sarah Well, no.

Mrs Bond Just as I thought. So you sit for Mrs Meredith improperly clad, regardless of whether *men* might come into the studio.

Sarah (*upset*) I don't. I just undo my blouse and draw it back over my shoulders.

Gran You could hardly expect Aphrodite to wear a collar and tie.

Mrs Bond (*icily*) Who?

Gran Aphrodite. It's a statue of Aphrodite, the goddess of love.

Mrs Bond (*with biting scorn*) Love! What the ancient Greeks called love was nothing but the lust of the flesh.

Gran In their eyes it was very beautiful.

Mrs Bond (*with repressed loathing*) It is not beautiful. It's filthy— degrading—animal behaviour!

Sarah Mother, don't get upset. I won't sit for it any more.

Mrs Bond Indeed you will not. I'll have no statue of Aphrodite with your features on it.

Gran You can't do that. Joan will be heart-broken.

Mrs Bond She can get another model.

Gran Only a complete philistine would say a thing like that. Let me tell you, my daughter is not in the habit of taking anything she can get. Last year she did a bust of the Prime Minister, and yet you imagine your daughter is too good for her!

Sarah Oh no, Mother didn't mean that.

Mrs Bond Yes, I did. Any decent girl is too good for a model of *that* creature!

Gran What do you know about Greek goddesses, an ignorant cook like you?

Sarah Oh, please don't upset her, Mrs Blackwell . . .

Mrs Bond I may be an ignorant cook but I know this: that when coarse, brutal men want a woman to respond to their demands, they give her an *aphrodisiac*! That tells me quite enough about Aphrodite, thank you.

Gran Of all the stupid arguments! Is that any reason for wantonly ruining a beautiful work of art?

Mrs Bond (*scornfully*) Beautiful!

Gran Yes, beautiful. But you're so riddled with nasty prudish ideas about sex, you have to spoil it and dirty it. I don't know how you ever came to have a child. It must have been the second virgin birth!

Mrs Bond (*shocked beyond measure*) Blasphemer!

Mrs Bond stalks out L, with a face of thunder

Howard (*mildly*) Well, you've properly thrown a spanner in the works, haven't you?

Gran Am I to be blamed for defending Joan's statue?

Howard Let's call it misplaced zeal. I'm sure Joan doesn't really mind what her statue is called. We might have persuaded her to call it *Naomi* or *Dorcas,* if you hadn't weighed in with such enthusiasm.

Sarah You shouldn't have said those things, Mrs Blackwell. I knew you would upset her.

Gran For heaven's sake, child, we're not all afraid of your mother. If a little bit of plain speaking is going to upset her, she'll have to *be* upset.

Sarah (*in great distress*) But she mustn't. You don't understand. It mustn't happen again. I couldn't bear it.

Gran Well, your concern for her is very touching. I only wish somebody cared as much whether *I'm* upset.

Howard Sarah, what d'you mean, it mustn't happen again? What mustn't happen again?

Sarah (*with difficulty*) Mother—she gets ill . . .

Gran Oh, lots of people feel sick when there's some sort of emotional crisis. It soon passes.

Sarah shakes her head dumbly

Howard Sarah, did something happen at your last place because your mother was upset?

Sarah (*obviously lying*) No. Nothing like that. I'd better put these cups away.

Luke enters R

Luke (*looking concerned*) Gran? I'm afraid I've got bad news for you. I've found Tiger Lily. She's—I'm afraid she's dead.

Sarah (*loudly*) Oh, no!

Gran Dead? My beautiful Tiger Lily?

Luke I'm afraid so, Gran. I'm terribly sorry.

Gran But . . . It must be a mistake. Where is she?

Luke Lying under the rhododendrons. Quite stiff!

Luke and Gran hurry out R

Sarah is trembling so that the cup she holds rattles in its saucer

Sarah How could she! How could she!

Howard Well, she was quite old, you know, for a cat. (*He takes the cup and saucer from her and puts them on the table*) You mustn't grieve, dear. She had a happy life.

Sarah But it's not fair. She didn't deserve to die. (*She hides her face in her hands and sobs*) All she'd done was sleep on the table.

Howard (*putting his arm round her shoulders*) She was twelve years old, Sarah. It was to be expected. Don't cry, my dear.

Sarah It was wicked! Wicked!

Howard There, there.

She leans against him, weeping, and he comforts her

Mrs Bond enters L and looks at them in surprise

Mrs Bond Is something wrong?

Howard (*relinquishing Sarah*) Yes, Tiger Lily's dead.

Mrs Bond The cat is dead? How? An accident?

Howard Possibly. More likely old age. Anyway, Luke broke the news rather suddenly and Sarah is distressed. It's very natural.

Mrs Bond Very natural. However, she must learn to control her feelings.

Howard A little sympathy means a lot to teenagers, Mrs Bond. I was comforting her as best I could . . .

Mrs Bond So I observed. But now she has her mother to comfort her so she won't need to trouble you any more, thank you, Mr Meredith. (*She holds open the door L*)

Howard Yes—well—that's all right, then. Try and take her mind off it, that's what I should do.

Howard exits L

Sarah sits at the table with her head on her arms and her shoulders shaking

Mrs Bond (*sarcastically*) So he was just taking your mind off it, was he?

Sarah He was comforting me. He has a soft heart.

Mrs Bond And you must have a soft head, to upset yourself so about a cat. (*She makes an attempt at comfort*) Why goodness me, it's not a tragedy. The creature had lived a long and happy life. It may have been spared much pain and suffering.

Sarah (*accusingly*) Is that why you did it? To spare her pain and suffering? Is that why you killed her?

Mrs Bond Killed her? Sarah! I did no such thing. How could you believe that of me?

Sarah Because you hated her. Because you said she should be put to sleep.

Mrs Bond If I said that I was speaking generally. I would never lift a hand against one of God's dumb creatures.

Sarah Lift a hand? Maybe not . . . But poison is different.

Mrs Bond Poison? What makes you think she was poisoned? (*She sits beside Sarah and stares at her*)

Sarah (*sobbing again*) I just know she was. It's so quick and easy. Poor Tiger Lily, one day sitting in the sun on the dining-room table, licking her beautiful, ginger fur, and next day stretched out cold and stiff under the rhododendron. Oh it was cruel of you. (*She hides her face*)

Mrs Bond (*suddenly suspicious, pulling Sarah's hands away from her face*) I thought so. You're not crying at all! Your eyes are as dry as mine! It's all play-acting, just like your father all over again. Seizing on any little domestic upset and building it up into a big dramatic scene. He should have been on the stage.

Sarah (*rebelliously*) I'm glad I'm like my father. He must have been a lovely person.

Mrs Bond That's what most people thought.

Sarah Well, he was warm and emotional. That's more human than someone who's cold and—and repressive. He had feelings and wasn't ashamed to show them.

Mrs Bond (*goaded into indignation*) He had no feelings for anyone but himself. What he showed was all pretence—like you and Tiger Lily. A bid to win sympathy.

Sarah I don't care. I can't help acting. One day I'll be famous.

Mrs Bond Your vanity will be your undoing, my girl.

Sarah (*bitterly*) Not if *you* can stamp it out. You just loved putting your foot down over that statue, didn't you?

Mrs Bond Sarah, speak with more respect or else go upstairs!

Sarah I'm going anyway.

Pause. Sarah glares at her mother who goes to adjust the saucepans on the cooker

You think you're pretty marvellous, don't you, because everyone admires your cooking, but it was *me* that got you this job.

Mrs Bond What do you mean?

Sarah They'd decided to give you the push, that first day, until Mrs Meredith saw me and wanted me for a model. That's why they took you on, not because you've cooked for ambassadors. Now you've wrecked Mrs Meredith's plans I expect they'll give us a month's notice.

Mrs Bond (*momentarily shaken*) If they do . . . But they won't. A good cook isn't cast aside like that. Mr Meredith said, only yesterday, that they haven't been fed so well for years. Mrs Meredith will get another model.

Sarah I shall hate her if she does. I shall hate her guts.

Mrs Bond Sarah Bond, keep a curb on your tongue!

Sarah (*sullenly*) If anyone needs to keep a curb on her tongue, it's you.

Mrs Bond What d'you mean by that?

Sarah Well, the way you carry on: bossing Luke and his father, quarrelling with the old lady. Anyone would think you wanted to be dismissed. Don't you like it here?

Mrs Bond (*after a pause*) Yes. We're very lucky to have a good position again.

Sarah Well then, why go round asking for trouble?

Mrs Bond (*with an effort*) You do right to rebuke me, Sarah. I have always been too outspoken for my own good. When people offend me I must remember my position and—be more humble.

Sarah It's nice here and I want to stay. I couldn't bear it if there was any
more—unpleasantness.
Mrs Bond Unpleasantness?
Sarah Like at Penfold Lodge. Last night I dreamed again about the fire. I
was terrified. Mother—you will be nice, won't you?
Mrs Bond Nice? I'll try not to be *provoked*, if that's what you mean. But
that woman uttered blasphemy. God will not let her go unpunished.
Sarah (*angrily*) Oh Lord, are we in for another *Holy War*?

*Mrs Bond turns on her and smacks her sharply across the face. They stare at
each other as—*

the CURTAIN *falls*

ACT II

SCENE 1

The same. The following Saturday morning

Sarah and Luke are sitting side by side at the table with text books open in front of them

Luke So you see that since XYZ and YZA are alternate angles, and since ZAY is a right angle, and bearing in mind that the three angles must add up to a total of one hundred and eighty degrees, we are now in a position to calculate the angle ZYA, aren't we? (*After a pause*) Aren't we?

Sarah (*who has not been paying attention*) Er—sorry, would you mind saying all that again?

Luke Yes I would. I've got other things to do besides your geometry homework. You're just not concentrating.

Sarah I know. It's dreadful. I can't think of anything except Mrs Blackwell —finding her lying on the grass beside her deckchair. My heart stopped beating. It really did. I thought she was dead.

Luke Well, she *wasn't* dead, and that was five days ago, so it's time you were able to think of something else.

Sarah How can you be so heartless?

Luke I'm not heartless. I've been as worried as the rest of you, thinking Gran was going to pass on at any moment. The fact remains that the doctor has pronounced her out of danger, so you can stop going round looking like an undertaker's mute.

Sarah It's been the most dreadful week. I don't know how I've lived through it. I kept praying to God not to let her die on bad terms with us.

Luke She wasn't on bad terms with you, was she?

Sarah With my mother she was. Didn't you hear about the row they had, last Sunday, when Mother found out about the statue of Aphrodite? Mother said Aphrodite was immoral and I was not to sit for it, and your grandmother said my mother had a dirty mind and Mother called her a blasphemer.

Luke It sounds like a real ding-dong. I'm sorry I missed it.

Sarah Mother was ever so upset. She hardly slept all night.

Luke I bet Grandmother slept like a top. She dearly loves an argument.

Sarah It must have upset her too. Why else did she have a stroke the next day?

Luke If it *was* a stroke.

Sarah Well, wasn't it a stroke?

Luke The doctor's very cagey and won't commit himself.

Sarah As soon as I heard her funny breathing I felt sure it was a stroke.

I'd just come back from school and I found her lying there on the grass. She'd been having tea in the garden and she'd been sick. (*She shudders*) It was terrible.

Luke Look, if it upsets you, don't keep thinking about it. She's all right again, quite perky in fact. Go up and see her if it'll reassure you.

Sarah Your mother thinks she was poisoned.

Luke (*startled*) Poisoned? That's ridiculous!

Sarah Well, she wouldn't let me wash up your grandmother's tea-cup, and I saw her putting pieces of cake into an envelope.

Luke Oh, really! It's all those stupid thrillers she keeps reading.

Sarah I heard her ask the doctor if it had been analysed yet and he said no, these things always take a long time.

Luke But who'd want to poison my grandmother?

Sarah (*after a fraction of a pause*) People can take poison by mistake. Lots of people eat toadstools in mistake for mushrooms, don't they?

Luke Yes, but you don't have mushrooms for afternoon tea.

Sarah I read a case in the newspaper where a whole family was poisoned because the mother used bulbs in mistake for onions in the stew.

Luke As far as I know, my grandmother was not eating onions for tea.

Sarah I know that, I'm simply giving examples of how people can make terrible mistakes.

Luke Talking of terrible mistakes, don't you think it's time you got this goemetry right?

Sarah (*with a sigh*) Haven't we finished question *one* yet?

Luke Well, *I* have, but your teacher might prefer it if *you* did a bit of work, too.

Howard enters L. *He goes and looks rather helplessly into the food cupboard*

Howard Does anyone know where Mrs Bond keeps the China tea? Mother fancies a cup and the doctor says it won't hurt her.

Sarah The tea's in that dispenser. (*She points to the fixture on the wall*)

Luke No, that's Indian tea. Gran can't abide Indian tea.

Sarah (*getting up*) Oh dear, I don't know where Mother keeps the China tea. Perhaps there's a packet in the dresser. (*She begins to search the dresser cupboards*)

Joan enters L *carrying a prescription*

Joan Has Mrs Bond gone shopping yet?

Sarah Yes, Mrs Meredith. She went about half an hour ago.

Joan Oh, what a pity. I was going to ask her to fetch this prescription from the chemist.

Sarah (*promptly*) I'll go. Please let me fetch it. I do so want to do something to help.

Joan That's very kind of you, dear. What about your homework?

Sarah I'll do it later. (*She takes the prescription*) I'll run all the way.

Joan (*smiling*) No need for that, my dear. The patient's not in danger any more.

Sarah No, but she must have her medicine or she might have a relapse. Luke, be a dear and put my books away, will you?

Luke No, I won't. Grandmother's not dying, so you can come and lend a hand. Where's your school bag?

Sarah I seem to have left it upstairs. Here, we can push the books in here for the time being, can't we?

Sarah puts the prescription on the table and she and Luke clear the books on to the bottom shelf of the dresser

Now, where did I put the prescription? Don't say I've lost it!

Howard It's here. (*He picks it up from the table*) Haven't you got a pocket or something to put it in? (*He hands Sarah the prescription*)

Luke (*examining a book he has found on the shelf*) Whose is this? *The Laws of Homoeopathy*?

Sarah Oh, that's Mother's. She's a great one for homoeopathy.

Luke You mean she goes about curing people with herbal mixtures?

Sarah Yes, sort of. She's had some wonderful cures.

Luke Fancy. I must tell her my symptoms sometime.

Sarah (*laughing*) Yes, you should. Her last employer used to get terrible toothache till she dosed him with belladonna.

Joan Belladonna? But that's deadly nightshade!

Sarah I know, but it did the trick. You'd be surprised what you can use to cure people with.

Joan Sarah, how long has your mother been practising this homoeopathy?

Sarah Oh, ages and ages. Actually she doesn't do so much now because . . . well, something happened at Penfold Lodge that discouraged her.

Joan Penfold Lodge?

Sarah That's where we were before we came here. Where's that paper? Oh, I've got it in my hand. Bye-bye, I won't be long. I'll take the short cut.

Sarah exits up R

Luke reads the book

Howard Joan, do *you* know where to find the China tea? Mother fancies a cup.

Joan Haven't we got any? Perhaps Mrs Bond is buying some. She'll be back soon and you can ask her.

Luke She's quite right. Look, for toothache it recommends belladonna. Or you can use mercury or in some cases aconite.

Joan But those are all poisons. Deadly poisons.

Howard My dear Joan, surely you know how homoeopathy works. These deadly poisons, as you call them, are taken in such minute doses that they couldn't hurt a fly.

Joan But if she practises this kind of medicine, she could lay her hand on all kinds of poisonous drugs, couldn't she?

Howard What are you getting at, dear?

Joan (*terribly worried*) I don't know. If only I could be sure.

Luke Mother thinks Grandmother was poisoned.

Howard Poisoned? Joan, do you seriously think that?

Joan Yes.

Howard But, *why* do you think so?

Joan (*unhappily*) The symptoms looked exactly like some I'd just been reading about in a murder story. Rapid breathing, low pulse rate, vomiting followed by coma. The victim had been poisoned.

Howard But darling, be realistic. Those symptoms could just as well indicate the onset of a stroke. You shouldn't let those sensational thrillers influence your imagination.

Joan That's what I told myself. But just to be quite sure I saved some crumbs of the cake she'd been eating and the dregs of her cup of tea. Doctor Smythe has promised to have them analysed.

Howard Well, honestly dear, I think you're wasting the doctor's valuable time.

Joan I hope so. But Mother says . . .

Howard What does she say?

Joan She told me that before she lost consciousness she was aware of a strange, tingling sensation in her lips and face—and then it began to go numb.

Howard Did she tell this to the doctor?

Joan Yes. He said that it *could* indicate a narcotic alkaloid poison, but it's not conclusive.

Luke I should think not, indeed. Mother, do you realize that if you're right, there's only one person likely to have done it?

Joan Of course I do. Mrs Bond.

Luke But why?

Joan They had a quarrel. According to Mother, some very bitter things were said. Mrs Bond called her a blasphemer.

Luke But blasphemy isn't a motive for murder.

Joan Not to you or me, of course. But to Mrs Bond it's an unforgiveable sin.

Luke But that would mean she's a nut-case!

Joan Well, you'd hardly call her normal, would you?

Luke A bit of religious mania is harmless enough.

Joan I tell you she's unbalanced. Why d'you think Sarah keeps begging us not to upset her mother?

Luke Does she?

Howard I must admit she does, quite often. And after the famous quarrel she was quite distraught. She said something about "it mustn't happen again". I tried to get her to explain what she meant and she said, "Mother gets ill".

Joan You never told me that.

Howard I never thought of it until this minute.

Joan "It mustn't happen again". That must be the incident at Penfold Lodge that she mentioned just now. You heard her say something had discouraged her mother from practising homoeopathy. Howard, we've got to find out what happened at Penfold Lodge.

Howard *We?* Look, this is *your* theory, Joan. I don't subscribe to it at all, and what happened at Penfold Lodge is none of our business.

Joan None of our business? When every meal that we eat might be prepared by a poisoner?

Luke For heaven's sake, Mother. The meals we eat are out of this world. Don't think of sacking Mrs Bond, I beg you.

Joan All right, Luke, I can see why you prefer to shut your eyes to my theory. Your stomach appears to rule your head. In Howard's case, it's his heart.

Howard My heart? I've no love for Mrs Bond.

Joan No dear, but you're very fond of Sarah, aren't you? She's almost like the daughter you always wanted. Oh, I'm fond of her too. She's a sweet child and I don't want her to get hurt. But, darling, you're a solicitor. You've got to be on the side of the law, and my mother nearly *died.*

Howard Very well then, let's look at this objectively. You maintain that your mother was poisoned by Mrs Bond as a direct result of their quarrel. You consider this provides the necessary motive. Next you must examine the means and opportunity.

Joan Opportunity is easy. On the afternoon in question, Mother was alone in the house with Mrs Bond. Luke was away, playing cricket.

Howard Where were you?

Joan In my studio, as usual, trying without much success to carry on with *Aphrodite* from some drawings I'd made of Sarah's head. I was there from about two o'clock until Sarah came running to fetch me at quarter to five. She'd just got back from school and found Mother lying on the grass in a coma.

Howard What was she doing out there?

Luke I believe she'd been having afternoon tea on the lawn.

Joan No doubt Mrs Bond carried it out to her on a tray. She had *every* opportunity.

Howard And the means?

Joan Well, I admit that had me puzzled, but now we learn about her dabbling in homoeopathy . . .

Howard Dabbling? Homoeopathy isn't witchcraft, you know. It's a respectable and honourable science.

Joan Let me see that book, Luke. (*She takes it and turns the pages, reading out names as they catch her eye*) Listen to this list of medicaments, then. Aconite; antimony; arsenic; belladonna; camphor; hemlock; digitalis; mercury—every other name is a well-known poison.

Luke They're not well-known to me—only arsenic. We don't all live on murder stories.

Howard We don't know that she has these medicaments in her possession.

Joan No, but I can find out if I'm quick about it. (*She moves towards the door* L)

Howard (*remonstrating*) Joan! You can't search her private belongings!

Joan I must, Howard. I shan't like myself for doing it, but I must.

Joan exits L

Howard Oh Lord, this is a pretty state of affairs.

Luke Surely you don't think there's anything in it?

Howard I wouldn't give it a thought, if it weren't for Tiger Lily.

Luke Tiger Lily? What d'you mean?

Howard I keep remembering things that Sarah has said. When you came
in and told us that the cat was dead, Gran and I assumed that she had
died of old age.

Luke Well, so she had.

Howard Sarah never thought so, not for a minute. She was in great
distress and she said something like "How could she? Tiger Lily didn't
deserve to die. All she'd done was sleep on the table." Looking back I
can see that she was blaming her mother for the cat's death.

Luke You mean, Mrs Bond poisoned Tiger Lily for sleeping on the table?
That's fantastic.

Howard Yes. Only, Sarah believed it, I'm certain.

Luke Well, even if it were true, it's a far cry from poisoning cats to
poisoning people. I shouldn't mention it to Mother or she'll have the
poor cat exhumed on the spot.

Howard No, after all, it can hardly count as evidence.

Luke (*after a pause*) Dad.

Howard Mm?

Luke Mother's changed, hasn't she? Ever since Gran was taken ill she's
been different.

Howard Well, she sat up for three nights by Gran's bedside, you know. It
makes people very tense and nervy.

Luke Nervy? No, it's not that. But she's not absent-minded any more.

Howard (*smiling*) Your mother has *never* been absent-minded.

Luke Never been . . . ? Here, come off it, Dad!

Howard I repeat, your mother has never been absent-minded. She has
always been *single*-minded. By that I mean that she pursues one train of
thought to the exclusion of all others. Most of the time her work is
uppermost in her mind and she gives no thought to anything else. But
in a crisis her work is put aside; she hasn't touched it for five days. All
her capacities are concentrated on the problem of your grandmother's
illness.

Luke Well, I've never seen her like this. I don't think I like it very much.

Howard No, I've got a nasty feeling that a good deal of unpleasantness
may occur before long and we shan't be able to dodge it.

Joan enters L *with a bottle of tiny white pills*

Joan I didn't have to search her belongings. Look what I found on her
bedside table!

Luke (*reading the label*) Aconite. Is that a poison?

Joan One of the worst.

Howard Joan, I've said it once but I must say it again. Those tiny little pills
don't contain enough poison to hurt a fly!

Joan Perhaps not, taken individually, but the bottle's half empty. Twenty
or thirty of these could probably do a lot of damage.

Luke And how did Mrs Bond persuade Gran to take twenty or thirty pills of aconite I'd like to know?

Howard I tried to persuade her to take an aspirin once, but I didn't succeed.

Joan She wouldn't take them knowingly . . . But if someone emptied half a bottle of them into a teapot and poured boiling water on to them, they'd dissolve, wouldn't they?

Luke My God, Mother, you ought to give up sculpture and write thrillers instead. I never heard such far-fetched nonsense.

Joan It's not. It's perfectly possible, isn't it, Howard?

Howard (*kindly*) Darling, it's an ingenious theory. I hate to have to point out the flaw in it.

Joan What d'you mean? Where is the flaw?

Howard Your mother always insists on making her own pot of tea!

Joan (*nonplussed*) Oh!

Luke That's right. It's like some sacred ritual and she's the high priestess. It's got to be her own special China tea and nobody else must touch it. Mrs Bond made it for her once, I remember, and got told off for her pains. So you see, Mother, it just won't wash.

Joan Wait a minute. Nobody but Mother drinks China tea. Why shouldn't the pills have been put into her special tea caddy and mixed up with the tea?

Luke Because Gran's not *blind*, you know. She'd hardly spoon a load of pills into the pot without noticing.

Joan (*getting excited*) That's just it, Luke. She doesn't use a spoon! It's a special kind of dispenser. You just hold it over the teapot and press a knob on the top and a measure of tea falls out into the pot. She wouldn't see a thing. Look, I'll show you Where's her little red tea-caddy?

Howard Well, I was looking for it just now, but it seems to have disappeared.

Joan Disappeared? (*She goes to the cupboard and hurriedly searches the shelves*) But it always lives here. Why should anyone move it?

Howard (*unwillingly*) I suppose—someone with a guilty conscience might get rid of it.

Joan Of course! Someone with a guilty conscience might get rid of it! And I'm willing to bet somebody did.

Luke Look out, she's coming up the garden path!

Joan Oh heavens!

Luke Are you going to accuse her?

Joan No. I'm a moral coward.

Howard You haven't got sufficient evidence to accuse her. It's all conjecture. You don't even know your mother was poisoned and I suggest you go very carefully with Mrs Bond, Joan. She's just the sort to have you up for slander.

Luke All the same, you ought to ask her a few questions. It's only fair to give her a chance to clear herself.

Mrs Bond enters R *with a basket on wheels, loaded with groceries, vegetables, etc.*

Mrs Bond (*looking questioningly at them*) Is anything wrong? Is Mrs Blackwell worse?

Joan No, my mother is continuing to improve. In fact, she was asking for a cup of tea and I came down to make it but her caddy isn't there.

Mrs Bond Mrs Blackwell's special tea is in the red caddy on the top shelf.

Joan I know it *should* be, but it isn't. See for yourself.

Mrs Bond (*looking for it*) That's odd. Who could have moved it?

Luke You haven't thrown it away, Mrs Bond?

Mrs Bond Why should I do that, sir?

Luke I've no idea.

Mrs Bond I'll send Sarah to the shop to buy some more China tea.

Howard Well, Sarah has already gone to the village to fetch a prescription. Don't worry, Mrs Bond, one of *us* will fetch some tea this afternoon. Mother can have a glass of milk. (*He gets milk from the refrigerator and fills a tumbler*)

Mrs Bond Very well, sir.

Luke Mrs Bond, do you know a lot about homoeopathy?

Mrs Bond (*very startled*) Homoeopathy, sir?

Luke Yes. This *is* your book, isn't it? (*He hands her the book*)

Mrs Bond (*suspiciously*) Where did you get that?

Luke Oh, you left it lying around. Sarah says you've worked some marvellous cures.

Mrs Bond Sarah exaggerates.

Joan takes the milk and exits L

Luke But you have cured people?

Mrs Bond Yes, I have—with the Lord's help. But I prefer not to talk about it.

Luke Oh, what a pity. But I suppose that's natural after what happened at Penfold Lodge.

Mrs Bond (*abruptly*) What do you know about what happened at Penfold Lodge?

Luke Oh, Sarah said something about it.

Mrs Bond What did Sarah say?

Luke Not very much. Nothing specific. She just sort of hinted that something unpleasant had happened.

Mrs Bond She had no right to say anything at all. What happened is over and done with. No good can come of opening up the subject again.

Luke Don't you think we have a right to know, Mrs Bond? After all, my parents took you on without any references.

Mrs Bond I explained the reason for that. They were burned.

Luke I know they were, but you could surely have asked your employer to write one out again, under the circumstances?

Mrs Bond (*turning to Howard*) Mr Meredith, is it your wish that I should be catechized in this way by your son? I understood that you were perfectly satisfied with my cooking?

Howard Yes, yes, indeed, more than satisfied. Come along, Luke, I need your help in the loft.

Luke All right, Dad. In any case, I can soon find out the answer to all the mystery tomorrow when I shall be at the scene of the crime.

Mrs Bond There *was* no crime. You have no right to . . .

Howard Luke, what are you talking about?

Luke Simply that I'm due to play cricket at Penfold St Mary tomorrow. The villagers are a chatty lot. (*He moves towards the door*)

Mrs Bond (*after a moment of indecision*) No! I'd rather tell you myself than have you listen to a lot of gossip that's been garbled out of all recognition. (*She begins to unload her groceries on to the table and during the following she packs some of them away*) I can only give you my version of the incident, of course. If you consult the vicar of Penfold St Mary, he will give you a very different account, I'm afraid.

Howard Never mind. Just tell it as it seemed from your point of view.

Mrs Bond While we were living at Penfold Lodge I was able to help the vicar on several occasions by prescribing homoeopathic pills for his ailments. He suffered very badly with rheumatism, and he said I had done him good where the local doctor had failed. This did not endear me to the doctor, as you can imagine.

Howard No, indeed. GP's are notoriously suspicious of homoeopathy.

Mrs Bond The vicar was a widower with two daughters, Marion and Jennifer. When their father praised my treatment they foolishly jumped to the conclusion that I had designs on their father.

Howard Designs, Mrs Bond?

Mrs Bond (*curtly*) Marriage. Their fears were quite groundless. Neither the vicar nor I felt an inclination towards matrimony, but gossip got around, as it so easily can in a small village. One day, Marion and Jennifer came and asked me to prescribe for *them*. One of them complained of warts and one of spots on the face. I considered their symptoms carefully and gave them pills of thuja and pulsatilla.

Howard Pills of——?

Mrs Bond Thuja and pulsatilla.

Howard Surely those are the names of plants in the garden?

Mrs Bond One is a tree. The other is a flower. Nothing could be more harmless than the medicine that is derived from them. The girls went away, giggling. A few minutes later, I had occasion to go down the lane myself and was amazed to see the girls rolling in a bed of stinging nettles.

Luke *Rolling* in the *nettles*?

Mrs Bond Yes, sir. When they saw me they looked guilty and ran off. The next thing I heard was that they had gone to the doctor that very evening and complained that my pills had brought them out in a rash. They also claimed that they had been violently sick.

Howard He believed them, no doubt?

Mrs Bond Of course. They were the *vicar's* daughters. There was quite an outcry, led by the doctor himself and I found myself ostracized by the people who I thought to be my friends. The younger people were particularly excited, led on by the vicar's daughters, who did not shrink from saying outright that I had tried to poison them. Rude words were painted on the wall and stones were thrown at my bedroom window. There were even anonymous phone calls of an extremely offensive nature.

Luke Not heavy breathing!

Howard Shut up, Luke.

Mrs Bond The persecution lasted for several weeks till eventually someone set fire to my room. No-one was hurt but a lot of my personal belongings were ruined. That was when I decided to leave and make a fresh start somewhere else. When I asked my employer for a reference, he refused point blank and said he was thankful to see me go.

There is a brief pause

Luke What an incredible story. It's like some medieval witch hunt.

Howard Are you quite sure it was stinging nettles they were rolling in?

Mrs Bond Yes, sir.

Howard Did no-one else see them rolling in them?

Mrs Bond No, sir.

Howard That's a pity.

Mrs Bond Yes, sir. It means you have only my word for it that it ever happened. (*She stares at him challengingly*)

Luke Did the girls recover from their warts and things?

Mrs Bond I don't know. I very much doubt if they took any of the pills I gave them.

Howard Suppose they did take some. Could the pills have made them sick?

Mrs Bond By themselves, no. If some sort of emetic was taken also, sickness could result. There are many ways of making oneself sick, sir.

Luke Yes, all you need to do is put your finger down your throat.

Howard Luke! Please! Mrs Bond, have you ever prescribed any pills for my mother-in-law?

Mrs Bond (*surprised*) No, sir.

Howard Nothing for, say, headache or indigestion?

Mrs Bond No, sir. I never heard Mrs Blackwell complain of either.

Howard If she had done, what would you have recommended?

Mrs Bond (*mistrustfully*) I can't say, sir. I'd need to know the cause.

Howard Might you prescribe aconite?

Mrs Bond (*on guard*) I might, sir. Why do you ask?

Howard Because I know that you have aconite in your possession.

Mrs Bond (*displeased*) Did Sarah say so?

Howard No. As a matter of fact, my wife saw it in your bedroom.

Mrs Bond (*rising*) Mrs Meredith has searched my room?

Howard (*embarrassed*) Certainly not. She had to go in for some reason— laundry, I dare say—and saw the pills on your table. She recognized the name from a book she'd been reading.

Mrs Bond I've been taking aconite for my catarrh. Nothing so sensational as the kind of book Mrs Meredith reads.

Luke In this book, someone put a load of pills in a tea-caddy and when the old lady made herself a pot of tea, she poured boiling water on them and they all dissolved. So she carried it into the garden and had a nice cuppa poison—only everybody thought she'd had a stroke.

Mrs Bond looks terrified. She tries to speak but cannot

What's the matter, Mrs Bond? Don't you think it's ingenious?
Howard You don't look very well. Do you want to go and lie down?
Mrs Bond No, I'm quite all right, thank you sir.

Sarah enters carrying her school satchel

Sarah I took the medicine up to Mrs Blackwell. She was looking quite perky—asked me to comb her hair for her.
Howard Is my wife with her?
Sarah No, she's telephoning in the hall. (*She goes to the dresser to pack her school books into the satchel*) Mother, since you don't want this tea-caddy any more, can I have it for school? (*She takes a small, red tea-dispenser from the satchel*)
Mrs Bond Sarah! Where did you get that tea-caddy?
Sarah You know where I got it. From the dustbin where you threw it away.
Mrs Bond But I never threw that caddy away.
Sarah (*all innocent surprise*) But I saw you. You put it in the dustbin the other morning and I rescued it and washed it clean.
Mrs Bond Sarah, what are you trying to do? You know I never threw away that tea-caddy.
Sarah (*upset and puzzled*) I don't understand. It wasn't a wrong thing to do, was it? Mr Meredith isn't cross with you for getting rid of it, is he?
Howard Sarah, it's the caddy where Mrs Blackwell kept her China tea.
Sarah (*all contrition*) Oh, I'm *so* sorry. I had no idea. Here, please take it back. I'm sure Mother didn't realize or she'd never have thrown it away.
Mrs Bond (*shrilly*) I tell you I did *not* throw it away!
Sarah Mother, don't get upset. You'll make yourself ill. Mr Meredith, *please* tell her that it doesn't matter.
Howard Look, let's forget about the tea-caddy for the time being.

Joan enters L, *rather dramatically*

Joan I've just been talking to Dr Smythe on the telephone. I think you ought to know that the results of the analysis have come through.
Luke Well?
Joan The cake crumbs were harmless, but the dregs of Mother's tea contained a strong dose of poison. There is no doubt that the poison was aconite!

Mrs Bond gives a harsh gasp

Sarah (*wildly*) Oh no! Not again!

Howard tries to restrain her. She seizes his arm frantically

She didn't mean to kill her! I'm sure she never meant to kill her! It can't be true! It can't happen all over again!

She collapses, weeping, into Howard's arms

Howard (*sternly*) Well, Mrs Bond, what have you to say?
Mrs Bond (*in a horrified whisper*) Nothing.

She stands, staring unbelievingly at Sarah, as—

the Curtain falls

Scene 2

The same. That afternoon. Sarah's books are still on the dresser and the satchel is on a chair near Gran, L

Gran, in a smart dressing gown, is seated in a chair down L. Luke is over by the window

Luke So you see, there could no longer be any doubt that she poisoned you, even if she only intended to make you ill, and Father had no alternative but to inform the police. He and Mother took her down to the police station in the car.
Gran Didn't she deny it?
Luke She said nothing at all. She was like someone in a trance. Sarah was quite hysterical, poor child. Mother gave her a sleeping tablet and put her to bed. I believe she's asleep now—and so should *you* be, Gran. The doctor would be horrified if he knew you'd come downstairs.
Gran Oh, fiddlesticks. I had to know what was going on and nobody came and told me. I've had enough of being in bed. One might as well be marooned on a desert island. I was simply dying of boredom, which I suppose was ungrateful of me having so nearly died of poison.
Luke Don't you think Mother was clever to see what was going on?
Gran Yes, but then Joan's like that. For years and years she lives with her head in the clouds, and then as soon as one of her loved ones is in any danger, she just takes off that side of her nature, like a garment, and becomes a person with drive, someone to be reckoned with.
Luke I was amazed.
Gran The last time it happened was when your Father had appendicitis. And before that, oh, years ago, when you were a little boy and you started to have nightmares. She left no stone unturned until she found out the cause.
Luke What *was* the cause?
Gran Heaven knows. Gluttony, I expect. I only remember that life was very uncomfortable and we were all thankful when she went back to her sculpture.
Luke Mrs Bond looked as though *she* was having a nightmare, when Sarah produced that tea-caddy. It was quite useless, her pretending that she'd not thrown it away. Anyone could tell she was lying desperately.
Gran Do you believe her story of the Penfold Lodge affair?
Luke Not the stinging nettles incident. No, it's obvious that she had a row with the vicar's daughters and when they came to her for pills she saw

her chance to pay them out by making them ill. I tell you, Gran, she's
got a twisted mind. What that poor kid must have gone through hardly
bears thinking about.

Gran She tried to warn us, didn't she?

Luke Repeatedly, but we didn't pay any attention.

Gran What will happen to her, if her mother goes to prison?

Luke I suppose she'll be put in some institution, or a foster home.

Gran And we shall be looking for another cook.

Luke Huh! I might have known it was too good to last.

Gran What did you have for lunch, Luke?

Luke Some bread and cheese and a lump of cake. What did . . .? Oh,
heavens, Gran, didn't you have anything?

Gran Don't worry, dear. I had a banana and some grapes and half a bar
of chocolate. You couldn't be expected to think of food at such a time.

Luke I'm awfully sorry, Gran. Let me get you something now.

Gran The only thing I really want, dear, is a cup of tea. I'm craving for one.

Luke There's only Indian, Gran.

Gran Oh dear, you know how I hate Indian tea. I suppose you couldn't
possibly go to the village for some China? It would only take ten
minutes on your bicycle.

Luke I'll gladly go, Gran, only—I don't like leaving you. I'm supposed to
be taking care of you.

Gran Well, so you will be, dear. You'll be ministering to my needs.

Luke You don't feel faint or anything?

Gran No, I feel very comfortable and rather thirsty.

Luke Right. Now, don't move from that spot. I've got some money. I'll
be back in a jiffy.

Luke exits R

*Gran looks around for something to read. She takes several exercise books
from Sarah's satchel which is within easy reach*

Gran "Chemistry"—ugh! "Maths"—oh, no. "English Essays" . . . (*She
opens "English Essays" and reads bits with a smile*) *My Favourite Play.*
"The best play I ever saw was *The Crucible*, by Arthur Miller. It made me
so excited, I couldn't sleep all night. It takes place in America, many
years ago when people believed in the Devil and religion was the most
important thing in their lives . . . The chief character is Abigail, a girl of
about sixteen . . ." (*She smiles and reads on in silence for a while, then
turns the page, frowns and reads aloud*) *The Death of Tiger Lily.* "In life,
Tiger Lily was a beautiful cat. Her coat was like orange velvet, shot
through with gleams of silver and white." (*Stirring in her chair, she reads
on in silence, then aloud again*) "She seemed to sense nothing wrong with
the saucer of food, but ate it in her usual manner, daintily, carefully and
completely. Then she stretched herself out in the sun. After a while, a
daring sparrow perched on the grass beside her. She watched it for a
moment, then tried to spring, but her movements, usually so swift and
graceful, had become clumsy and slow. She managed to stagger to her

feet, only to fall over again. Her sides heaved with the effort to breathe. She struggled to be sick, but without success . . ." (*She goes on reading with a look of amazement. After a moment, she closes the book and stares in front of her, pondering and worrying. Then she opens the book and reads aloud again*) "The best play I ever saw was *The Crucible*, by Arthur Miller. It made me so excited I couldn't sleep all night." My God! (*She covers her face with her hand*) My God!

After a moment Sarah comes in, wearing tight trousers and a clinging top

Sarah (*subdued*) Hello, Mrs Blackwell. Are you feeling better?

Gran stares speechlessly at her for a moment

Gran Yes, I'm a lot better, thank you. How are *you* feeling, Sarah?

Sarah I don't know, really. I'm trying not to think about—what happened. That's why I put on these trousers, I suppose, to convince myself that I'm somebody else. Mother doesn't know I have them. I got them in a jumble sale but I've never worn them before because Mother says it's immodest. (*Her manner denotes an uneasy self-control*) I shall take them off before they bring her back from the police station. (*She sits at the table opposite Gran*) Mrs Blackwell, do you think they'll bring her back?

Gran I don't know, Sarah. Deliberate poisoning is a very serious crime. They might charge her with attempted murder.

Sarah (*quietly*) Then she'd have to go to prison. And what would become of me? Where would I live?

Gran The authorities would arrange something.

Sarah I don't want to live in any other place but this. I love it here. D'you think Mr Meredith would let me stay on? He likes me, you know; he's very fond of me. I think he's always wanted a daughter.

Gran Yes, I think he has.

Sarah I could do the cooking, you know. I've learned it all from Mother. And I could sit for Mrs Meredith to carve my head and I could have a room of my own . . .

Gran And wear trousers all the time? You've got it all worked out, haven't you?

Sarah You think I'm wicked to be planning ahead, don't you? It doesn't mean I've forgotten poor Mother already. I could weep when I think of her. But I always knew in my heart that it would come to this one day. There were other incidents before Penfold Lodge, you know, and although I tried hard to believe in Mother's innocence, I gradually saw that she had a kind of sickness—in her mind—so it wasn't really safe for her to be at liberty. (*Shakily*) I've got to try to convince myself that she's better off in—in custody.

Gran Sarah, tell me what happened at Penfold Lodge.

Sarah Oh, that was awful, though the victims weren't as ill as you were. But *that* started with a quarrel too. You see, the vicar was a widower and his two daughters got it into their heads that Mother wanted to marry him, so they came to Mother and pleaded with her to leave him alone. I felt sorry for Mother, they made it so painfully clear that they didn't fancy her for a stepmother, and she was very hurt and upset about it. Not long after that, they came and asked Mother to prescribe some pills for Marion's warts and Jennifer's spots.

Gran Wasn't that an odd thing to do?

Sarah Odd? Why?

Gran Well, if they disliked her so much, why would they ask her a favour?

Sarah Oh, it was their father's idea. They did it to please him.

Gran And what did she give them for their warts and spots?

Sarah I don't know, but it made them violently sick and it caused a severe rash. You can imagine what a fuss there was. The whole village turned against us. The doctor said some very horrible things, and one or two girls who I thought were my friends turned really spiteful. There were anonymous letters and telephone calls, and people turned their backs on us in the street. Everyone sided with Marion and Jennifer. They were such nice little girls.

Gran How old were they?

Sarah About twelve and fourteen, I should think.

Gran Did they see *The Crucible* too?

Sarah (*taken aback*) I beg your pardon?

Gran I read in your essay book that you saw a play called *The Crucible* and found it exciting.

Sarah Yes. I went with a school party. Marion and Jennifer weren't old enough.

Gran It's a remarkable play, is it not?

Sarah (*fervently*) Wonderful.

Gran It made a strong impression on you, didn't it?

Sarah Yes. Some of the girls were really frightened.

Gran I'm not surprised. It's a frightening idea that a young girl with a look of childlike innocence can accuse her elders of crimes they never committed, and have them brought to trial and convicted all for her own amusement and spite. How many people were actually hanged as a result of her lies?

Sarah Oh dozens. All the people who had ever annoyed her in the smallest way.

Gran What was the girl called—was it Abigail?

Sarah Yes. Abigail. It's a wonderful part. I'd give anything to play that part.

Gran And you'd do it very well. You have that trusting, innocent look about you. And you're quite an actress, I believe.

Sarah (*pleased*) Oh, do you think so?

Gran Indeed I do.

Sarah I'd better get these books packed up. (*She starts packing the books into her satchel*)

Gran Yes, I should. It doesn't do to leave evidence lying about.

Sarah Evidence? What d'you mean?

Gran I'm incurably nosey, Sarah. I didn't stop at your essay on *The Crucible*. I read the next one, too.

Sarah The next essay?

Gran *The Death of Tiger Lily.*

Sarah Oh. (*She stands very still, staring at Gran*)

Gran What did your teacher say about it?

Sarah She said I had a remarkable imagination.

Gran That wasn't imagination, Sarah. You saw that cat die.

Sarah That's not true.

Gran You watched every stage of its death with close and loving attention. And of course, you had good reason to watch it closely since it was a kind of run-through—a dress rehearsal, you might say, for something on a bigger scale.

Sarah You're not talking sense, Mrs Blackwell. I don't think you're well enough to be up.

Gran I may be a bit weak in the legs, Sarah, but my brain is as good as ever. My tea was definitely poisoned with aconite, and because your mother hates me, and because she keeps aconite pills by her bedside, and because she has a guilty look about her, Howard and Joan have rushed her off to the police station. It's a pity they didn't stop and consult me first. I could have told them two important facts: (a), that if homoeopathic pills could be used to poison people's tea they would not be so easily obtainable and (b), that aconite in its truly lethal form grows wild by the riverside, under the name of monkshood, or wolfsbane as no doubt you know.

Sarah I've never heard of it.

Gran It's quite a pretty plant. It has a tall spike of yellow flowers . . .

Sarah (*involuntarily*) Blue.

Gran Ah! So you know it!

They stare at each other. Sarah realizes she has almost given herself away

Sarah What if I do? It doesn't prove anything.

Gran That's true, it doesn't. And of course there are no witnesses to this conversation, so anything you say now you can deny later. So just to satisfy my curiosity, Sarah, how *did* you do it? It was remarkably clever, however it was done. Did you soak the flowers?

Sarah Of course not. If—if I *had* wanted to poison someone I should have used the root. That's the part that really matters. It's a sort of browny-grey. If you grate it with a cheese-grater it looks near enough like China tea.

Gran So you grated it into my tea-caddy and went gaily off to school, knowing that sooner or later I would pour boiling water on to it and drink a strong infusion of aconite. Ye gods, if I'd let it brew a while longer, I doubt if I'd be sitting here talking to you.

Sarah That may be how it was done, but you can't prove *I* did it! It was Mother you quarrelled with, not me. Why should I want to poison you?

Gran I don't know. Maybe you think that everybody over the age of seventy ought to be killed off.

Sarah That's nonsense. There's no reason on earth why I should want to harm you.

Gran A motiveless crime does seem odd, I grant you. (*She ponders a* *moment*) Shall I tell you what I think your motive was? The whole cunning plan wasn't aimed at me at all. The fact that I got poisoned was only incidental to the main object. And that was, to *get rid of your mother!*

Sarah stares at her, wide-eyed and speechless

Yes, I feel sure I'm right. Everything was done to implicate her right from the start. Your pathetic anxiety not to let us upset her. Your dark hints about what happened "last time". You sowed the seeds and waited for one of us to quarrel with her. It was bound to happen sooner or later, your mother had a way of stirring up strife. You had a little practice go on Tiger Lily and that no doubt gave you confidence.

Sarah It's all lies.

Gran But you shouldn't deny something so remarkably clever. The whole plan was quite brilliant, and that last stroke, saying you'd seen her throw the tea-caddy into the dustbin, couldn't have been neater.

Sarah You've no right to suggest that I'd hurt my mother. I love her.

Gran Oh no, you don't. You hate her. She's strict and severe while other parents are easygoing. She forces the Bible down your throat if you dare to look at yourself in the mirror. She won't let you have a room of your own as long as there's a young man in the house. She makes you eat frugal meals while the rest of us dine royally. She won't let you wear trousers or modern clothes. One way or another she's cut you off from all the jolly things of life, and the final indignity came when she forbade you to sit for Joan's statue of Aphrodite. That was the last straw that sealed her fate, wasn't it?

Sarah (*passionately*) It wasn't fair! Nobody has ever admired my head before! And I loved sitting for Mrs Meredith. What did it matter if Aphrodite was immoral? But she had to put a stop to it, just like she put a stop to everything I wanted to do. She's made my life wretched, utterly wretched. She deserves everything that happens to her!

Gran (*with a sigh*) I dare say it has been hard on you. Your mother must be a very difficult person to live with.

Sarah (*sullenly*) It's because I'm like my father, in looks and in character. And she's afraid I'll go the same way as he did.

Gran Which way did he go?

Sarah To the bad, poor devil. Strong drink and loose women. I reckon she drove him to it. In the end he couldn't stand her preaching and he left home.

Gran But Sarah, she's only strict with you because she loves you and wants to protect you.

Sarah (*with a small smile*) I know. And that'll be her downfall.

Gran What d'you mean?

Sarah (*coming to sit by her*) To protect me, she'll let them go on believing she did it. She'll even confess in the end, rather than let me go to prison. Mothers are like that, aren't they? The strongest force on earth is a mother's love for her child. (*Contemptuously*) Isn't that a wonderful thought.

Gran Don't say any more. I don't want to hear such things from you.

Sarah Why not? I can say what I like here, without any witnesses. I can always deny it afterwards.

Gran Don't be too cocksure, my child. What *I* say will be believed.

Sarah (*meaningly*) If you get the chance to say it!

Gran (*startled*) What do you . . .?

Sarah Aren't you taking rather a risk, sitting here talking to someone you suspect of trying to poison you? There's nobody here but us, remember, and I'm a lot stronger than you in your present condition.

Gran I don't think you'd be so silly as to try and hurt me while your mother isn't here to take the blame. You'd simply be giving her an alibi.

Sarah I could easily give you a blow on the head with a—with a rolling pin, and say you fell over and hurt your head. People often fall down when they're weak and old. It would just be a tragic accident. I should run all the way to the police station and arrive in a hysterical condition. I'm very good at a hysterical condition.

Gran You sound half hysterical now. Take a grip on yourself, child, and face reality. As things stand now, you could only be sent to a remand home. You haven't yet committed the unforgiveable crime. You can make a fresh start.

Sarah Yes, but not with you still on the scene. I want to stay on here. I could be rid of mother and I could be like a daughter to Mr Meredith. It would be wonderful, if only you were dead.

Gran Sarah, it wouldn't work. You can't force circumstances to obey your will.

Sarah I have up till now. Abigail did.

Gran Abigail ran away in the end. Why don't you run away, too?

Sarah (*rising*) No. I want to stay here.

Gran (*nervously*) Keep away from me!

Sarah You're scared.

Gran I am not. If I were scared I'd go and telephone the police.

Sarah Go on then. Ring them now. Tell them you don't like being left alone with a little schoolgirl. Go on, I won't stop you.

Gran I don't intend to stir from this chair.

Sarah Good. That makes it easier.

Gran Easier?

Sarah (*holding her by the shoulders, from behind*) To *strangle* you! I could, you know. Your throat doesn't look very big.

Gran (*striving to remain calm*) If you strangle me, the marks on my throat will give you away.

Sarah That's true. But I believe there are pressure points, here at the sides —(*She moves her hands to encircle Gran's neck*)—where I could *squeeze* you to death and leave no trace.

Gran (*tensing herself to resist*) If you do, I warn you I shall put up quite a struggle. You won't get away unmarked.

Sarah What sort of a struggle could an old woman like you make? You're too scared. I can feel you trembling. Your heart's banging away like a piston, isn't it? And your legs are shaking so that they wouldn't support you. You shouldn't really be up from bed, should you? It's enough to cause a relapse. If you were to drop down dead with a heart attack, the doctor would sign your certificate without a second thought. (*Shouting suddenly in Gran's ear*) Wouldn't he?

Gran (*shaken, but grimly maintaining composure*) Sarah, I know perfectly well what you're trying to do. You're trying to frighten me to death because you haven't the nerve to use violence. But I don't intend to have a heart attack to save you from justice. I intend to stay alive and see that you get your just deserts.

Sarah (*furiously*) Damn you, then! Damn you to hell! (*She turns away in a rage and stands at the window for a moment, twisting the curtains. Suddenly she turns back with a look of desperation*) The car's coming up the drive. They're back already. As far as they know it was all Mother's doing, so I warn you, if you say a word about me you'll be sorry.

Gran Fiddlesticks! I shall tell them everything.

Sarah If you do—I shall tell them about Luke! About what he did to me!

Gran What d'you mean?

Sarah He raped me! He did, I tell you!

Gran He did no such thing, you lying little bitch!

Sarah Yes he did. Last Wednesday, in the cornfield. I shall tell it in court—I shall give all the details. How I struggled—how he hurt me—how I was ashamed to tell my mother. He'll have to leave Cambridge. You'll all have to go away and live somewhere else. You'll never live down the disgrace. So if you care about your precious family, you'll bloody well shut up about this afternoon!

Gran (*in a horrified whisper*) Where did you learn such villainy?

Mrs Bond enters L, *followed by Howard and Joan*

Sarah (*incredulously*) Mother!

Mrs Bond Well, Sarah?

Sarah They set you free?

Mrs Bond Yes, Sarah, they set me free.

Sarah (*weeping on her shoulder*) Oh thank God!

Joan Mother, are you all right?

Gran Yes, dear. Quite all right. Sarah and I have been having a very interesting little talk.

Joan A little talk! Oh, Mother, if you did but know!

Gran As a matter of fact, I *do* know. What surprises me is that *you* seem to know.

Joan We know who tried to poison you. Mrs Bond told us.

Gran Mrs Bond told you? Well, Sarah, so much for the strongest force on earth.

Sarah I don't believe it. Mother would never tell . . . It's lies she's told you. It's all lies!

Mrs Bond No, Sarah, I told them the truth.

Sarah (*incredulously*) And they believed you?

Mrs Bond Not at first. But luckily the police doctor has considerable knowledge of homoeopathy, and he knew that my aconite pills couldn't possibly have had such effect.

Sarah (*desperately*) That doesn't matter. You picked monkshood from the riverside! I saw you!

Howard (*with much sadness*) Sarah, don't. It's no good. I saw you with your arms full of monkshood, the day before Tiger Lily died, but like a fool I never realized that monkshood and aconite and wolfsbane are all the same thing. If I had, I might have remembered that poem. I might have prevented this from happening.

Mrs Bond (*very sad and bitter*) Don't reproach yourself, sir. She'd have found out some other way, no matter what you did. She's been playing around with poisons ever since she could read. That's why I locked up your books, Mrs Meredith, for fear she'd find some new method of doing harm.

Sarah It's not true. She's making it all up.

Howard Sarah, the police rang up your last school. The headmistress told us that you were expelled for lying, stealing poisonous chemicals and corrupting the younger girls. The police also rang up the vicar of Penfold St Mary and he admitted that his daughters had since confessed that they lied. They admitted it was all a plot devized by you.

Sarah (*hissing*) The little bitches! I made them swear on the Bible that no-one should ever know!

Mrs Bond *I* knew.

Sarah You knew?

Mrs Bond Oh yes. I knew you had organized those foolish girls to persecute me. They'd never have thought of it on their own. And it had that touch of drama that you can never do without.

Sarah (*puzzled*) You never told.

Mrs Bond No. Nobody was hurt, that time. I wanted to give you a chance of a fresh start. I prayed to God to help you to cast out the wickedness that was in your heart. But now—now that these terrible things have happened, I know that God wants the responsibility to be mine, not His. The casting out must be done by me.

Sarah (*pitifully*) But Mother—I'm your child.

Mrs Bond That is something I shall suffer for all my life. Once before I listened to my motherly instinct and covered up for your sins. I was wrong to do so and Mrs Blackwell nearly died. I made my decision on the way to the police station and God will give me strength to go through with it.

Sarah But—what is going to happen to me?

Mrs Bond You will be taken to a remand home. There is a policewoman waiting in the hall. Come upstairs with me now and we will pack your case.

Mrs Bond exits L

Sarah pauses, looking forlornly round her. The others look away

Luke enters R, *with a packet of tea in his hand*

Luke There's a police car outside. What's happened? Sarah, tell me.

Sarah (*sadly*) I'm going home.

Luke Home?

Sarah That's what they call it.

Luke Is your mother going too?

Sarah No. I haven't got a mother any more. (*She walks slowly to the door* L, *then she turns back*) I shan't always be in a remand home, you know. One day I'm going to be famous. You haven't heard the last of me—not by a long chalk.

Sarah exits

CURTAIN

FURNITURE AND PROPERTY LIST

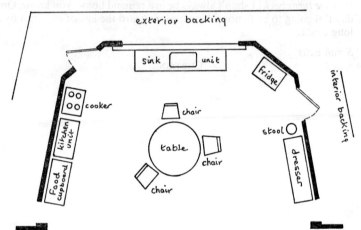

Only essential items are listed. Further dressing may be added at the director's discretion

ACT I

SCENE 1

On stage: Electric cooker *On it:* filled kettle (practical).

Kitchen unit. *On it:* electric toaster (practical) containing toast. *On wall above:* calendar, tea-dispenser containing tea

Food cupboard. *In it:* packet of corn flakes

Table. *On it:* jug of milk, 4 cups and saucers, 4 plates, library book

3 wooden chairs (or 2 wooden chairs and a rocking chair)

Welsh dresser. *On shelves:* cups, saucers, plates, bowls, teapot, tumblers etc. *On dresser top:* bowl of sugar, tray. *Inside drawer:* spoons

Stool

Refrigerator (practical)

Sink unit. *In sink:* basin containing burnt frying pan. *By sink unit:* tea towel hanging on hook

Pot plants on window sill

Sketch pad and pencil (for **Joan**)

Off stage: Letter, newspaper **(Luke)**

Books, including a complete volume of Shakespeare, Keats's poetry and an atlas **(Luke)**

Parcel of fish **(Gran)**

£5 note **(Mrs Bond)**

Personal: **Mrs Bond:** apron

SCENE 2

Strike: From table: any remaining items except milk jug and sugar bowl
             From sink: basin containing used crockery and burnt frying pan

Set: 2 saucepans on cooker
             Jar of instant coffee, spoon, coffee pot on kitchen unit
             Cups and saucers on dresser shelves to replace those used
             Pie in dish in refrigerator
             Empty basin in sink

Check: Kettle filled

ACT II

SCENE 1

Strike: From cooker: saucepans
             From kitchen unit: jar of instant coffee, spoon

Reset: Tray and bowl of sugar on dresser top
             Cups, saucers and coffee pot on dresser shelves
             Jug of milk in refrigerator

Set: Exercise book, text books open on table
             Homoeopathic book on bottom dresser shelf

Off stage: Prescription **(Joan)**
             Bottle of tiny, white pills **(Joan)**
             Shopping basket on wheels. *In it:* groceries, vegetables etc **(Mrs Bond)**
             Satchel. *In it:* small, red tea-dispenser; (for Scene 2) exercise books for
             "Chemistry", "Maths" and "English Essays" **(Sarah)**

SCENE 2

Strike: Shopping basket on wheels
             Small, red tea-dispenser

Re-set: 2nd chair L near **Gran.** *On it:* satchel

Off stage: Packet of China tea **(Luke)**

LIGHTING PLOT

A kitchen. The same scene throughout

ACT I, SCENE 1   A morning in September
To open: Overall effect of bright Autumn sunshine
No cues

ACT I, SCENE 2   A morning in September
To open: As Act I, Scene 1
No cues

ACT II, SCENE 2   An afternoon in September
To open: Overall effect of afternoon Autumn sunlight
No cues

EFFECTS PLOT

ACT I

Scene 1

Cue 1   **Joan:** ". . . no good at telling lies."   (Page 6)
Door bell rings loudly

Cue 2   **Howard:** ". . . if it's not too late."   (Page 9)
A door is closed firmly off L

ACT II

No cues

MADE AND PRINTED IN GREAT BRITAIN BY
LATIMER TREND & COMPANY LTD PLYMOUTH
MADE IN ENGLAND